THE
ULTIMATE
SALES
LETTER

SECOND EDITION

THE ULTIMATE SALES LETTER

**Boost your sales with
powerful sales letters,
based on
Madison Avenue techniques**

DANIEL KENNEDY

Adams Media Corporation
Avon, Massachusetts

Published by
Adams Media, an F+W Publications, Inc.
57 Littlefield Street, Avon, MA 02322 U.S.A.
www.adamsmedia.com

ISBN: 1-58062-257-7

Printed in Canada

J I H G F

Library of Congress Cataloging-in-Publication data available
upon request from the publisher.

This publication is designed to provide accurate and authoritative information with regard to the subject matter covered. It is sold with the understanding that the publisher is not engaged in rendering legal, accounting, or other professional advice. If legal advice or other expert assistance is required, the services of a competent professional person should be sought.
— From a *Declaration of Principles* jointly adopted by a Committee of the American Bar Association and a Committee of Publishers and Associations.

This book is available at quantity discounts for bulk purchases. For information, call 1-800-872-5627.

Since its first publication in 1991, this book has inspired and guided tens of thousands of people in diverse businesses and sales activities in creating and using "the ultimate sales letter." Here are a few of their remarkable stories:

"I first read *The Ultimate Sales Letter* in July 1991—and have reviewed my highlighted, underlined, and dog-eared sections dozens of times. I shamelessly and repeatedly use Section #6, and it has added buckets of money to my political fundraising letter. I bought an extra copy for the National Director of the Libertarian Party—he also swears by it!"

—Michael Cloud, Nevada

"This afternoon my wife and I were being poled down a jungle waterway so we could see 20 different kinds of monkeys and 100 different kinds of parrots . . . the alligators are slithering into the water, and I'm reading your book, *The Ultimate Sales Letter*—quite a scene! So you can quote me: *The Ultimate Sales Letter* is more interesting than a jungle full of monkeys and a river full of alligators!"

—Don Berliner, California

"I have followed your examples, used your three-step letter campaign, and had tremendous results—I spent $1500 and created $20,200 in income! Thanks!"

—Randy Thomas, Real Estate Quest, Illinois

❖

"Carefully following the instructions in *The Ultimate Sales Letter*, I put together a long sales letter, for the purpose of securing appointments with top decision-makers in my industry. In over 20 years in this business, I've never sent anything longer than a one-page letter, and frankly, I doubted your approach. But this time, instead of fighting through secretaries, and making follow-up call after follow-up call, these prospects were calling me. I had an outstanding response. So far, I've written over $50,000 in new business from mailing only 2500 letters."

—John Cummings, Michigan

❖

"Could direct-mail work for a little store like ours? Following *The Ultimate Sales Letter*, we sent out a four-page letter to all the people in our area, followed by three post-cards, and we brought in over 100 new customers, and immediately got back our little investment ten times over."

—Mary and Walter Bruchan, Washington

CONTENTS

INTRODUCTION
TO THE FIRST EDITION

One of the most challenging things to me about a sales letter (as opposed to direct interaction with a customer) is that it requires you to think about the customer's needs and desires well in advance. As Dan Kennedy makes clear in this excellent book, when you master the skill of moving a potential customer to action through a finished sales letter, you take that preparatory work and put it into action—and truly understand salesmanship as both an art and a practice. I first learned about Dan's remarkable skills when we began working with him on "infomercial" scripts for our company. (An infomercial is essentially a 30-minute sales letter brought to life on television.) We have used many of the techniques outlined in this book to reach hundreds of thousands of customers—and the result has been over $20 million in sales in our first year of business!

Once you learn the fundamentals Dan sets out in this book, you'll find yourself recognizing good sales copy wherever you go—and also recalling Dan's advice on motivating potential customers. Whether you're watching a television commercial, glancing at the mail that crosses your desk, or even listening to a salesperson, you will see that the truly compelling sales work conforms to the simple guidelines in *The Ultimate Sales Letter*. You'll find yourself making improved persuasive presentations not just in print, but in your everyday activities, too.

At Guthy-Renker Corporation, we spend a lot of money to reach consumers. Considering the size of our commitments, there is little room for error. We have to seek out the finest writers available: professionals who understand the fundamentals, are experienced, and can deliver results. We work with Dan Kennedy regularly because he meets all these qualifications—and because he keeps us from trying to reinvent the wheel. Quite simply, Dan's ideas—the very same ideas outlined in *The Ultimate Sales Letter*—work spectacularly.

And that's good news for you if you plan on reaching customers on paper. The 1990s, after all, will be the era of the sales letter: recent research indicates that the average cost of a one-on-one sales call now exceeds $350. While the costs of old-fashioned marketing go up, the availability of niche marketing technology becomes increasingly attractive. With computer databases, we can cluster target audiences by their geo-demographic traits, and use a wide variety of methods, studies, and services to define and reach out to our ideal customers. Mass marketing is out. Target marketing is in, and those who can write targeted copy to specific customers will hold the competitive edge in the years ahead. The sales letter is the ultimate target marketing tool!

The real power of a sales letter comes when we transfer our excitement and convictions directly to the reader in a way that motivates action. Dan Kennedy shows how to incorporate such impassioned delivery into every sales letter—no matter what product, service, or offer it promotes.

Dan Kennedy is a masterful teacher and a compelling writer. Most important, though, is this: he can produce results. I wish you every success in your application of his winning methods to your own sales letters.

Greg Renker
President
Guthy-Renker Corporation
Palm Desert, California

Guthy-Renker Corporation is famous for its TV infomercials featuring Tony Robbins, Victoria Principal, Vanna White, and others.

Note from the author: Greg Renker wrote this introduction for the first edition of this book, published in 1991. At that time, Guthy-Renker Corporation had been a continuing client of mine for three years. Now, in 1999, Guthy-Renker Corporation is still a client, with a relationship that has continued over a total of 11 years. Although relationships of this duration are unusual in business in general, this is not unusual for me. In fact, over 80% of all clients who retain me once for consulting or direct-response copywriting, do so repeatedly. And to put that in a frame of reference, keep in mind that, to write a primary sales letter or direct-mail package and follow-up letters for a client, my fee typically ranges from $15,000 to $25,000 plus a royalty linked to usage and results. I mention that not to brag, but to emphasize the value of what you are about to read and work with, because in this book you have the exact same process, and the most reliable strategies that I use to do that work.

SECTION I

Before You Write a Word . . .

WHAT TO DO BEFORE YOU START WRITING

One sage said, "Writing is easy. You just sit down at the typewriter, slit your wrists, and give blood." Well, it certainly isn't as bad as *that*.

I am convinced that just about anybody can learn to craft very effective sales letters. I have no opinion one way or the other about your ability to write the next Great American Novel, a cookbook, a children's storybook, or a Broadway play. (I've written a country-and-western song: "I Love My Wife but I Forgot Where I Live." But that's another story.) I do have great confidence in your ability to write a successful sales letter, for two basic reasons.

First, you presumably know more about your business, product, service, and customer than anybody else. Getting that understanding is the hard part. Writing with that understanding is easy. When I or some other freelancer is brought in to write sales letters, we have to do our best to acquire that understanding before we can even begin writing. That takes a lot of time and effort and energy, and there's still no way we can get exactly the same full understanding, the same intuitive insights from experience, that you must have in your chosen business.

This is a tremendous advantage and you, my friend, possess it.

Second, my own background tells me that just about anybody can learn to do this. I am a high-school, not a college, graduate. I did not go to work in the mailroom of some ad agency and learn the trade of copywriting from experienced, seasoned pros while pulling myself up the corporate ladder. In fact, I got my first paid copywriting assignment while still a senior in high school and opened my own ad agency two years later, with no relevant experience or education behind me. I just did the same things you can do:

1. I got books like this one, devoured them, kept them handy, and used them as guides. I sure wish there had been a book exactly like this one, with a step-by-step system, but there were and are plenty of other good ones.

2. I used my own insight, intuition, powers of observation, and common sense.

3. I translated what I knew (and what I kept discovering) about selling and communicating in person to the task of selling and communicating in print.

4. I built up huge "idea files"—samples of ads, mailings, and sales letters. These are called "swipe files" by pros, and that is exactly what they are used for— to swipe ideas from. You do not need much creativity to write letters; you only need to be adept at recycling and reorganizing ideas, themes, words, and phrases.

In spite of my lack of formal education or training in this field, I've developed literally thousands of sales letters for my own business enterprises as well as for hundreds of clients, and over 90% of them have been successful. Many have been tested against "control" letters crafted by much more educated "professionals," and mine have won. Last year, I was called in by a company to write a letter to test against one already being used, which had been written by one of the top three or four pro copywriters in America. I went up against this widely recognized, much admired, very highly paid guru, and I beat the pants off him. I do not tell you all this to brag; I tell it so that you will realize that you can do it, too. I'm self-taught. You can be self-taught.

Also, for most of your purposes, you do not need the same skill level that I or other top, professional copywriters have painstakingly developed. In most situations I work in, I'm putting together sales letters that will compete against other sales letters written by other top pros, but you will more likely be competing in an environment where top-flight pro copywriters do not prowl.

One great copywriter, John Francis Tighe, quoted the philosopher Erasmus, "In the land of the blind, the one-eyed man is king."

Since this book was first published, I've received literally thousands of "success stories" from people in every imaginable business or sales career, who have used this book as their guide, put together a sales letter from scratch, and achieved desirable and profitable results. Some have gone on to great proficiency. Several have become consultants and copywriters.

I recognize that a large part of your success will depend on your confidence to do something. The mechanics are all here for you. But you have ultimately to go from your first read of this book to the act of following its steps, getting sales letters prepared, and into the mail.

Here are some general ideas that will help you get started:

1. Don't be intimidated by the idea or process of writing. There's no magic or genius or Harvard degree required.
2. Recognize the value and power of your unique understanding of your business, products, services, and customers. You may find it useful to build reference lists or stacks of 3-by-5-inch cards—"What I Know About Our Customers . . . About Our Product . . ." and so on.
3. Assemble and organize ideas and samples in a "swipe file"; assemble and organize good reference materials.
4. Think "selling." If you have successful sales experience—terrific! Writing a sales letter is much more akin to getting down on the living room floor with Ma, Pa, the kids, and the dog and selling a vacuum cleaner than anything else. If you don't have a "selling mentality," get one! Get some good books on selling. (See my Web site, *www.dankennedy.com*, and this publisher's Web site, *www.adamsmedia.com* for some ideas.) Never forget that a sales letter is a sales presentation in print.
5. Write. Don't worry about writing a letter from start to finish. Just write blocks of copy and stack them up. A lot of great sales letters are eventually put together with scissors and tape (or by cutting and pasting using a word processing program). Write!
6. Avoid perfectionism. In most businesses, for most purposes, you don't need a perfect sales letter to get good results. If you follow the guidelines in this book, have something worthwhile to offer, and understand your customer, you may not put together the perfect sales letter, but I'll bet you do put together one that works.

Many people believe that the great, persuasive sales-letter writers just sit down at their computers and let the priceless prose flow! I have known two or three who can do this, but most do not. Most professional sales-letter writers give themselves the advantage of careful, thorough preparation, and you should, too.

Remember, the more you write, the easier it will get. Just about everything you do easily now was once difficult to do. From fear to confidence; difficult to easy; incompetent to competent—that's a movement we repeat over and over again throughout our lives. It's the process that gives life meaning, that prevents boredom, burnout, and depression. It's good for you! It builds healthy self-esteem, which prevents unhealthy addictions and destructive behavior. Gaining new competence in any skill, such as writing sales letters, automatically enhances your confidence in all other areas! In short, you're going to find the ability to craft effective sales letters to be a major asset personally and for your company.

SECTION II

The System

Step

1

GET "INTO" THE CUSTOMER

An old adage says that you can't understand someone until you've walked a mile in their shoes.

It's a good adage. We entrepreneurs, for instance, would be much better off if each of our elected representatives had to spend a couple of weeks every year running a small business, struggling to meet a payroll, and filling out a slew of government forms. The people trying to work their way out of the slums would be much better off if each of our elected officials had to go live with them for a week or two every year. And our farmers would get some of their problems solved if each of those same officials had to spend a week every year working on a farm. A number of well-run companies require their top executives to take customer complaint calls periodically, open and read mail from customers, even get out into the stores and deal with customers face to face.

The goal is *understanding*. To persuade someone, to motivate someone, to sell someone, you really need to understand that person.

How easy is it to miss? Not long ago, I wrote a TV infomercial script (essentially, a sales letter that comes to life) selling a home-mortgage-related product. The script called for the spokesperson to walk into a living room, saying, "Here, in a typical American home. . . ." The producer filmed this line with the spokesperson stepping into a white-carpeted room with a grand piano as its centerpiece! Out of touch, out of touch! Admittedly, most marketers are never that far out of touch with their customers or prospects, but make a mental note: the more in touch you are, the more probable your success. In my Copywriting Mastery Seminar (which hundreds of people paid $2000 each to attend),* I provide a special checklist of smart questions to ask about your customers and prospects. That checklist is reprinted here, as a very valuable "bonus" with this book.

MY "10 SMART MARKET DIAGNOSIS AND PROFILING QUESTIONS"

1. What keeps them awake at night, indigestion boiling up their esophagus, eyes open, staring at the ceiling?
2. What are they afraid of?
3. What are they angry about? Who are they angry at?
4. What are their top three daily frustrations?
5. What trends are occurring and will occur in their businesses or lives?

---

*My "Copywriting Seminar in a Box" is available at 1-800-223-7180 or *www.kimble-kennedypublishing.com*.

6. What do they secretly, ardently desire most?
7. Is there a built-in bias to the way they make decisions? (Example: engineers = exceptionally analytical)
8. Do they have their own language?
9. Who else is selling something similar to thcm, and how?
10. Who else has tried selling them something similar, and how has that effort failed?

So, Step 1 in our system is to analyze thoroughly, understand, and connect with the customer.

In some cases, you may have a lot of demographic and statistical data about your customers or prospects available from your own records or from the vendors of the mailing lists you are using. You might (and probably should) know the ages, incomes, hobbies, and political affiliations of the people you're writing to—even what magazines they read regularly. Hopefully, you can even get beyond this data and gain a "feeling" for these people. If you have none of this, if you have nothing but zip codes, I'd suggest getting into your car and driving slowly, several times, on different days, through the neighborhood with one of those zip codes, to try to get a feel for those people. Or, if you're marketing to businesspeople, attend their meetings, read their trade journals.

Dr. Bill Harrison of the Top Performance Center in California, an optometrist by training, has done a great deal of research into the various uses of "visualization" and has received tremendous media recognition for his work with top athletes, helping them to improve their performance. Dr. Harrison has helped such notables as Billy Caspar improve his golf game and George Brett play better baseball. Bill says, "If you can really see it, you can get it." I believe that, and I believe this extension of it: if you can really see your prospect, you can communicate successfully with him in print.

I've spent 20 years working with the visualization techniques developed by Dr. Maxwell Maltz, author of the 30-million copy bestseller, *Psycho-Cybernetics*, and I use those techniques—like "Theater in Your Mind"—to visualize my letter's recipients as living, breathing, thinking, feeling, walking, talking human beings. I visualize their day's experience. How did it start out? What did they do when they first arrived at the office? Do they get their mail presorted? Opened? From an "in" basket? Hand-delivered? When do they get it? Where will they stand or sit when going through it? At that time, what else are they thinking about? Preoccupied with? What do they worry about, complain about, secretly wish for, enjoy? Through this stretch of my own imagination, I try to become one with my letter's recipients, so I can anticipate their thoughts and reactions. If you don't have enough information and experience to do this, you must get it! I try to accept assignments to write sales letters only to types of prospects I know well. But given an assignment aimed at people I didn't understand, I'd go get that understanding.

Once I had to write a series of letters to realtors. Well, I've never been in the real-estate business and, at the time, I knew no more about it than the typical man on the street does. What did I do? I went to the public library and read back issues of the specialized trade magazines that realtors subscribe to. I read several books on real estate. I noticed that one of the big real-estate franchise companies was in town that week for its convention, so I went and hung around the hotel's lobby and bars and eavesdropped on conversations. I got myself to the point where I could visualize myself as a real-estate broker.

Once you've begun that process of identification, you'll be in a good position to determine what your letter's recipient wants. Write these items down in order of priority.

WHAT IS MOST IMPORTANT TO YOUR READER?

There is a classic sales legend about the hot-shot salesman pitching a new home heating system to a little old lady. He told her everything there was to tell about BTUs, construction, warranties, service, and so on. When he finally shut up, she said, "I have just one question—will this thing keep a little old lady warm?"

Each time I've gone shopping for a personal computer, I've seen the same selling error repeated over and over again in the computer stores I've visited. These salespeople tell me everything about what's important to them, but they never slow down long enough to find out what's important to me.

The mistake is even easier to make in crafting a sales letter, because there's no possibility of corrective feedback from the customer during the presentation. That's why you must determine accurately, in advance, what their priorities are. And you must address their priorities, not yours.

I was asked to write a corporate fund-raising letter for the Arthritis Foundation's annual telethon in Phoenix. In examining samples of letters other nonprofit organizations sent to corporate donors, I noticed that they all had this failing in common; they talked at great length about their own priorities—what they needed the money for, how it would be used, how funds were low, etc.—but they hardly addressed the donor's priorities at all. So I visualized myself as the business owner or executive being banged at by all these worthy charities' pleas and asked myself: "If I were to give, what would be important to me?" I came up with this list:

1. What benefit to me or my company justifies the cost?
2. Who else had picked this drive to contribute to? (How can I validate my judgment?)
3. How would I get the money to give? (What budget would it come out of? What other expense would have to be reduced to afford this new one?)

With that list in mind, I wrote the letter reproduced on the following pages. It garnered a response of only half of one percent, but the responses were from important new donors—one of whom contributed $13,000. This one new donor's contribution covered about half of all the costs of the local telethon that year. Perhaps most important, every expert associated with this project believed that such a letter would not work at all. Their previous experiences told them so. And in terms of return-on-investment, it was the most successful fund-raising effort ever mounted by this local chapter. So why did this letter work where others had failed? Because it directly addressed the interests of the recipient, not the sender!

Get a fix on the prospect/customer/client, and on his or her desires; failing to do so will undermine all your other efforts.

_____ Director of Marketing

Dear _____:

Special, **highly effective TV exposure** at half the ordinary cost, even a smaller fraction of the ordinary cost—even free! Yes, it is possible.

Our annual **ARTHRITIS FOUNDATION TELETHON** has moved to CHANNEL 10 (Phoenix' CBS affiliate), and we are offering an expanded, more flexible, more creative range of Sponsor Opportunities to businesses of all sizes in the valley.

Many corporate sponsors last year actually participated spending little or no money—the funds were raised through fund-raising events or promotions involving their employees or customers. For example, one major corporation used several Employee Promotions, and raised over $50,000. A small company used a Bowl-A-Thon with their employees, employees' family members and friends and raised $5,000. Both received excellent exposure on the Telethon. **AND THIS YEAR, THE OPPORTUNITIES ARE EVEN GREATER!**

There are many different Sponsor Programs available including several that give you a competition-free exclusive position. Sponsors are needed for each hour for the phone banks; for the Interview Area, where guests are interviewed by celebrity hosts; for table banners; and much more. There are even a few 1 and 2 minute Video Presentation Opportunities (company exposure) available. In all cases, representatives of your firm come on the show for you, your people and your products. We will also assist you every step of the way with your employee fund-raising event or other promotion, to raise the funds for your sponsorship. There really is no good reason not to participate.

As a sponsor, you'll be showing your concern for the community, in connection with a situation that, at one time or another, will affect over 35% of all families! Arthritis is one of the most common, frustrating, debilitating diseases. It is understandably of great concern to a great many people. Also, the Arthritis Foundation has an excellent track record in terms of appropriate use of funds for research and education (rather than organizational overhead). We believe that real cures for arthritis are just around the corner; you can help get us there!

With our Telethon on Channel 10, we will benefit from their superior production capability, involvement of their popular celebrities, and advance promotional opportunities. Our Telethon will be on for several hours immediately before and again immediately after an NBA Basketball Game, which we believe will increase our viewership. And, of course, we're mixing our live, local show with a "feed" from the National Telethon, featuring major Hollywood entertainers. Everything points to our highest, most responsive viewership ever!

You'll be in good company, too, with local and national sponsors like: **Thrifty, Sears, Allstate, Greyhound, Prudential and Procter & Gamble.**

To summarize, you have an opportunity to . . .

1. Help a good, worthy cause
2. Gain valuable TV exposure and publicity
3. Get all the benefits with little or no money out of your present budget—we'll work with your employees to raise the funds!
4. Possibly have exclusive position, if you act quickly
5. Have complete, step-by-step assistance from our staff

Why not give me a call; let's arrange a meeting where I can personally explain the different "standard opportunities" available and then "brainstorm" with you about the best way for your business to participate. There's no obligation, of course, and certainly no pressure, but, together, we just may figure out the perfect situation for your business.

Thank you for your consideration,

Joel L. Beck
Telethon Chairman for the Arthritis Foundation

JLB/va

Letter reprinted with permission of Dan Kennedy (writer) and Joel Beck, former telethon chairman, Arizona.

Step

2

GET "INTO" THE OFFER

Just as you try to crawl inside the letter recipient's mind and heart, you want to crawl around in your product or service, too.

If you're writing a letter to promote a product, get the product, use it as the consumer would, play with it, test it, take it apart and put it back together, even demonstrate it to others as a salesperson would. If you're writing a letter to promote a service, use it yourself if possible. Go talk to those who do use it. Talk to people who use a competitive service. If you're writing a letter to promote a special offer, do everything possible to analyze that offer. Try it out on people. Find out if they understand it, if they're intrigued by it.

BUILD A LIST OF PRODUCT/OFFER
FEATURES AND BENEFITS

I like to put each item on separate 3-by-5-inch cards, so I can shuffle them after I've written them all out and sort them according to importance. This works better for me than a list on a sheet of paper. Sometimes I tack the cards up in a vertical row on a bulletin board in my office so it's easy for me to keep looking at them as I write. This is essentially a brainstorming exercise. You can do it alone, aided by product literature, the product itself, even competitors' advertising and literature. Or you can do it with a group of participants. Either way, the idea is to list every possible feature and benefit, then organize them by importance.

Note that I said "features and benefits." It's amazing how easily people fall into talking about the features of their product or service, instead of the benefits it provides. I find myself constantly reminding our clients: "People do not buy things for what they are; they buy things for what they do."

Now, here is an advanced copywriting secret, courtesy of my friend Ted Nicholas: the use of "the *hidden* benefit." Ted has personally sold over $200 million worth of how-to books via direct-response ads in magazines and newspapers and via sales letters, and retired relatively young to Switzerland on the proceeds, so he knows a thing or two about salesmanship-in-print. Ted often looks for what he calls the hidden benefit to emphasize. This means it's not the obvious benefit; not the first benefit you think of, yet one that is of profound importance to your customer.

I'll give you an actual example. Pamela Yellen, the CEO of the Prospecting & Marketing Institute, based in Santa Fe, New Mexico, and I were conducting a multi-day seminar for her clients—corporate executives and general agents from life insurance companies—about new methods of recruiting agents. Even though the attendees had paid a very high per-person fee to be there, most had traveled great distances, and the subject was of critical importance to them, we both noticed that on breaks, what most of them were talking about was where they were going to go play golf that evening when the seminar let out, the next morning before it started, or the day afterward. Both Pamela and I made note of how important it was to these clients of hers to get out on the golf course.

This led to one of the most profitable ads Pamela has ever written and run in her own industry's trade journals, with the headline: "Puts Recruiting On Auto-Pilot So You Can Go Play Golf!" The entire ad is reproduced on the following page. As you'll see, it sells the system we devised for insurance agent recruiting, but it does so circuitously, by emphasizing the hidden benefit: you'll get that job done with less time invested, so you can spend more time on the golf course.

| 22 |

3

CREATE A DAMAGING ADMISSION AND ADDRESS FLAWS OPENLY

This may seem strange to you at first, but identifying the flaws in your product, service, or offer is a big step forward toward making the sale!

By acknowledging the flaws, you force yourself to address your letter recipient's questions, objections, and concerns. You also enhance your credibility.

FIGURE OUT WHY THEY WON'T RESPOND

People are damned contrary creatures! You present them with a perfectly good offer and they still don't respond—why not? I think it was Yogi Berra who said, "When people don't want to come to the ballpark, there ain't nothing that can keep 'em from not coming." Well, there are lots of reasons not to come to the ballpark.

Again, I like to use 3-by-5-inch cards and put a reason for not responding on each card. I try to think of every possible objection, concern, fear, doubt, and excuse someone might use to keep from responding.

I talked with a doctor about a particular product being marketed through the mail by a company competitive with my own. The doctor told me that he had received at least a dozen sales letters from that company, had read them, and was interested in the product; I knew he had the financial ability to buy. So why hadn't he? He told me that he felt the offer was too good to be true, and that made him skeptical about everything said about the product. If the marketer had anticipated that reaction and answered it somewhere in his letter, he would certainly have increased the response to his mailings.

An acquaintance of mine (not a client) is in the phone-sex business. This means he has 900 numbers and Internet sites, advertised in raunchy magazines, that men can call or download, paying by credit card, to indulge in sexual fantasy conversations with women. Admittedly, this is not the most elegant business; the mere mention of it may offend some readers of this book, yet his experience provides a great object lesson. He told me he tripled the response to his ads by adding one sentence. Now, think for a minute. As difficult as it may be, try to use your imagination to visualize the customer who will spend $20 to $30 for this type of diversion. Who is he? We know he has a credit card. We know he is presumably alone, maybe lonely. And he has purchased a certain kind of magazine. Anybody come to mind yet?

Try: "traveling salesman." Now, what would be his priorities concerning this "purchase"? Wouldn't one be secrecy? He certainly wouldn't want "Phone Sex" or an adult Web site fee to appear on his monthly Visa bill for his wife, company comptroller, or accountant to see! So the sentence that tripled response was: "Discreetly billed to your credit card as 'XYZ Supply Company.'"

These are examples of the importance of anticipating and confronting the reasons not to respond.

HONESTLY ASSESS THE DISADVANTAGES OF YOUR OFFER AND FACE THEM

Every product, service, and offer has some unattractive points. Nothing's perfect, and everybody knows that. By admitting and openly discussing the drawbacks to your offer, your "credibility stock" goes way up on most of your letter recipients' charts. This is sometimes called "damaging admission copy." Consider this example, from a sales letter sent to area residents by a small Italian restaurant:

> . . . if you want waiters in tuxedos with white linen cloths over their arms, menus with unpronounceable words all over them, and high-priced wines served in silver ice buckets when you go out for Italian food, our little restaurant is not the place to come. But if you mostly want good, solid, home-cooked pasta with tasty sauces made with real vegetables and spices by a real Italian Mama, and will trade white linen for red and white checked plastic tablecloths, you'll like our place just fine. If you're okay with a choice of just two wines, red or white, we'll give you as much of it as you want, from our famous bottomless wine bottle—free with your dinner. . . .

This restaurant owner took competitive disadvantages and turned them into a good, solid, "fun" selling story.

4

GET YOUR SALES
LETTER DELIVERED

Early in the process of putting together your sales letter, you need to think about getting the finished letter into the hands of people who can respond.

There is a very real, significant mail nondelivery problem in this country. Various studies and audits conducted by the Postal Service, the Direct Marketing Association, and others indicate that 10 to 30% of properly addressed third-class mail never reaches its intended recipients! I believe the problem is even worse. Postal employees actually discard or deliberately destroy huge quantities of what they perceive to be "junk mail." The best counterattack options for the sales-letter sender have to do with envelope design, but the design option you select directly affects the letter's theme and copy, so this selection must be an early step in the system.

THE OBSTACLE COURSE

Maybe there were even earlier signs of this ugly problem, but the first time it was brought to my attention explicitly was November 18, 1987, when a Reuters news service article appeared in the *Los Angeles Times* headlined: "Postman Convicted of Destroying Mail." Here it is, verbatim:

> MINNEAPOLIS—A postman who said he was tired of hauling around stacks of junk mail was convicted Monday of trying to destroy 93 bundles of it.
>
> A federal court jury found Stephen Spoerner, 36, guilty on three counts of destroying mail. He could face up to 15 years in jail and a fine of up to $750,000.
>
> He was arrested last year when a nursing home janitor found undelivered stacks of advertisements and solicitations dumped in the incinerator. Postal inspectors said Spoerner dumped the mail three times and undercover agents caught him in the act the third time. When he was arrested Spoerner said, "I only did this on occasions of heavy mail volume."

End of article, but just the beginning of the story. Consider, for example, *Target Marketing* magazine's report (April 1989) on the conviction of a Florida postal employee who had dumped nearly half a million pieces of mail in a landfill on his property. Although less pervasive, the dumping activity even extends to first-class mail.

Even before I read these pieces, I'd been charting for some time some erratic, unexplainable patterns and incidences of total nonresponse from certain geographic areas to mailings that worked successfully everywhere else. I had asked myself: "Can it be that only the people of St. Louis hate this offer? Is there a credit card blight in St. Louis?" And I had finally concluded that the mail simply never got there.

And I had heard rumors—like the story I got from a reliable postal-system insider about the "junk drop" in the Bronx, in New York City. A "junk drop" is postal-employee slang for a known, shared place where these criminal postal carriers can safely discard mail (mounds of mail!) rather than deliver it. This particular junk drop was an abandoned apartment building. The only reason it was discovered was that there was so much undelivered mail accumulated there, in floor-to-ceiling piles, that spontaneous combustion took place in the July heat and the whole building exploded into flames.

In the ensuing couple of years, the problem has gone from quiet industry gossip to public knowledge, largely thanks to the dogged efforts of the Direct Marketing Association. An August 1989 article in the trade newspaper *DM News*, headlined "Deliverable Bulk Business Mail Often Goes in Garbage," brought us this cheery news: the U.S. Postal Service's own audit found properly addressed mail frequently destroyed at all of the 111 post offices and 12 bulk mail centers checked! Between that year's audit and the previous year's, the problem had gotten worse, not better. The postal sites where substantial amounts of properly addressed, deliverable mail were found discarded en masse, usually in Dumpsters, increased from 76% in 1987 to 84% in 1988. In other words, an increasing number of postal carriers, loading-dock workers, and postal-station managers are joining in the collusive, deliberate destruction, and nondelivery of mail. In addition to this wanton destruction and dumping, substantial quantities of third-class mail gets damaged in handling and processing. On the day the audit team visited the San Francisco Bulk Mail Center, 22 hampers of damaged mail were sitting in the "delayed section," and four more hampers were labeled "trash." This same audit also revealed "mountains of third-class mail delayed" at bulk mail centers—48,000 pieces in Pittsburgh and seven hampers of mail in Dallas. The length of time it had been delayed was unknown.

YOUR TAX DOLLARS AT WORK

I could go on. This situation is absolutely abysmal, and the hierarchy of our postal system has been reluctant to cop to it or do anything about it. The point is that before you can get the deathless prose of your newborn sales letter read, you've got to figure out how to get the darned thing delivered.

I even know of incidents where dumping of quantities of first-class mail has taken place. I have charted the same weird patterns of nonresponse to mass mailings sent first class as I have for bulk. So, while mailing first class, preferably with an actual stamp rather than a meter imprint, tremendously improves your odds of delivery, it's still no guarantee.

I'm told that, recently, the postal service has been aggressively working on this problem and succeeding at reducing deliberate nondelivery. Improvements have apparently been made. I think the problems are less pervasive today than when I first wrote this book. But the risk of nondelivery remains. I even have some clients who now profitably use bulk mail. As recently as 1998, however, I know personally of two very significant instances of deliberate nondelivery that sabotaged entire mailing campaigns. The worst part of this problem is that you might never know that your mailing was done in by nondelivery. So I still consider this when making all the decisions about the outside of the mailing piece.

Often I design envelope exteriors or mailer formats with fooling the postal worker in mind. The same design ideas that increase odds of delivery also seem to increase the odds of getting it opened and looked at, but, frankly, my big concern is successfully conning the postal workers!

I first discovered quite by accident that this could be done, and the story is instructive. These days, imitation overnight-express envelopes are quite common; you've undoubtedly seen them and probably received at least a few. But some years ago, I think before they existed or, at least, when they were still rare, I chose that format for a mailing. It was for a company called General Cassette Corporation, and we designed a red-white-and-blue General Express Letter package. It featured pictures of jet airplanes and wording like: URGENT—OPEN IMMEDIATELY. The mailing was going to a thousand of the company's best clients and prospects, and it was going via cheap bulk mail.

The first thing that happened was that the supervisors at the Phoenix Bulk Mail Station refused to accept the things. I had to call our attorney who got a directive from Washington, D.C., ordering the local station to accept the mail.

I quickly understood their reluctance. The morning after the bulk-mail drop, we started getting telephone calls from as far away as Boston and New York—from people who had received delivery of our Express Letter in the middle of the night, by the post office's express mail people! We were ultimately able to track over 150 units that were handled and delivered as express mail—15% of the mailing. Much of the rest was apparently handled as first class, based on the quickness of the customer response. And virtually all of it got there. In fact, an 82% response rate was achieved. I can just see a batch of eight or nine arriving at the Duluth post office: veteran carriers look at it and grumble, "Must be some new kind of express mail. As usual, nobody tells us anything. Better jump in the Jeeps and get these delivered pronto!"

The lesson I learned from that experience was that it is possible to con the postal workers into doing their job and delivering my mail. I've kept it in mind every time I've assembled a mailing since then. I suggest you do the same. Here are a few strategies that seem to work consistently:

FIRST CLASS VS. BULK

Bulk's no bargain if you're hit with a 20% and up nondelivery factor, and my own experience indicates this may well be the norm. If you can possibly adjust the economics of your business to justify first-class postage, that's what you should use.

LIVE STAMPS VS. METER INDICES

The basic principle behind these strategies is that postal workers are least likely to dispose of mail they believe the recipients are expecting. Live stamps seem to suggest that only a small number of pieces were mailed and that they may be expected correspondence rather than "junk mail." Incidentally, automated stamp-affixing machines are readily available.

INDIVIDUALLY OR INK-JET ADDRESSED ENVELOPES

A gummed white label is a dead giveaway in most cases.

Recently, I had an interest in a business mailing as many as 25,000 hand-addressed envelopes a week. A whole neighborhood of stay-at-home moms picked up boxes of envelopes at the office each Monday, took them home, addressed them, were paid piece-meal, and brought them back on Wednesday. We knew from testing that it made enough of a difference in response to justify this extra effort.

THE SNEAK-UP APPROACH

A plain white envelope with no business name; only an address with no name or a person's name as the return address; no teaser copy; individual or ink-jet addressing; and a live stamp—all this makes your mailing look like a letter, not advertising or junk mail. It then stands the highest possible chance of completed delivery. Given that design and first-class postage, I'd give it a 98% chance of getting there and getting opened.

INTIMIDATING IMPRINTS

"Audited Delivery . . . Verified Delivery . . . The Information You Requested Is Enclosed . . . Important Documents Enclosed . . ." Imprints or affixed gold seals with this kind of wording seem to work well.

ELABORATE, INTIMIDATING ENVELOPE DESIGNS

The "express letter" appearance has lost its impact with postal workers, although it still works well with recipients. Very "official looking" designs now seem to work best. The design shown on the following page, from a fund-raising letter sent by the Republican Presidential Task Force, is an excellent example of this type of design.

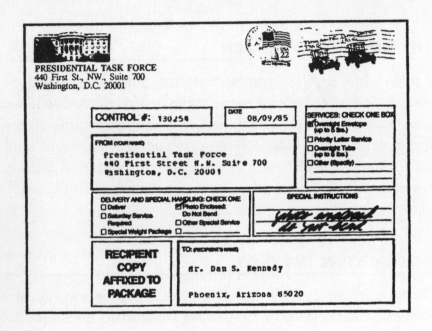

5

GET YOUR SALES LETTER LOOKED AT

Let's optimistically assume that the lion's share of your mail survives the determined destructiveness of our postal system and actually arrives at its intended destination. Now what?

Just about everybody throws out some mail unopened. Letters that do get opened and looked at have only a quick heartbeat to survive the sort, avoid the wastebasket, and earn the attention and interest of the recipient.

The best and most succinct advice I ever got on this subject is from a true direct-marketing genius, Gary Halbert. Gary says, "Picture the person you've sent your sales letter to with a stack of mail in his hands, sorting through that stack, standing next to a wastebasket." You might write that up as a sign and post it on your wall: America sorts its mail standing over a wastebasket.

Wow! That is an insight worth a great deal of money. Think of it this way: People prejudge their mail, just as they do other people, places, books, and so on. That may be unfair or unreasonable, but it really happens.

If you're sending sales letters to businesspeople, consider that the mail may be screened by an assistant. If you survive that "cut," then your recipient sorts the envelopes—not the actual letters—standing over a wastebasket.

Even I, a mail junkie and collector, have days and sometimes weeks when I am just too busy to open and read every piece of mail that crosses my various desks. I receive mail at three places: my post-office box, my office, and my home. During busy times, when I go to the post office and extract a three- or four-day accumulation from my box, I literally stand next to the waste can. I throw out as many envelopes as I can unopened. The rest go in my briefcase, to take home and read later, except for a piece or two that look personal or especially important, which I open and read immediately. At the office, pretty much the same ritual takes place.

Let me give you an example of how big an impact this can have. We have a business that mails extensively to doctors, and, over the years, I've tried every kind of envelope look you can imagine. By far, the mailings that pull best are sent in "plain Jane" envelopes without our company name on them but, instead, a doctor's name and return address. These envelopes are not screened by staff. They get opened by the doctor. The response to these mailings versus the same letters sent in different, more "honest" envelopes is sometimes as much as 300% higher!

Mailing to consumers at their homes carries a different set of problems. First of all, it is my admittedly informal observation that in most households most of the mail is sorted and handled by the woman, not the man. And today's extraordinarily busy working woman is ruthless in handling this mail. Much of it hits the trash without seeing the light of day.

So, how do you get your sales letter opened? The same strategies I just described for fooling postal employees also serve to motivate recipients to open the envelope. In addition, different sizes and colors of envelopes can add impact and gain attention. If you are going to use a devious strategy, the most important thing to remember is that you must quickly fulfill the envelope's promise inside. For example, when we mail with a doctor's name as our return address, we enclose a little scratchpad-size "lift letter" from that doctor that says: "The information presented here has been of immense value to me and I thought it might interest you, also. The Publisher asked me to let you know how much I've gained from his service and I was glad to do so. You'll do yourself a favor by reading everything enclosed. Sincerely . . . ." Similarly, if your envelope says "Personal" outside, there had better be something "personal" inside. Unfulfilled envelope promises destroy the credibility of everything enclosed and everything you have to say. Fulfilled envelope promises work to enhance your credibility.

6

GET YOUR SALES LETTER READ

In person-to-person selling, there is a little formula taught almost universally: "AIDA," which stands for: Attention, Interest, Desire, Action. This is the orderly process of a sale. So, once you've gotten the letter recipient's attention, you must work to develop his or her interest.

FROM ANNOYING PEST TO WELCOME GUEST

One warm afternoon I was at home alone, sitting at my kitchen counter, a large iced tea in hand, talking on the telephone with an important client in another city. The doorbell rang. I ignored it. It rang relentlessly. I ignored it. Then the uninvited, unwanted pest pounded on the door. "Damn," I said to myself—but I still tried to continue my conversation. Suddenly there was someone banging on the sliding glass door behind me; at this stage it was a contest of wills and I refused to even turn around and look. Then he was back banging on the front door. I finally excused myself from the conversation and went to the door to get rid of this guy.

He was a passing motorist trying to tell me that the shrubs along my backyard wall were in flames!

Suddenly this guy was elevated in status from annoying pest to welcome guest! Clearly, he was on my side: "Get the hose going—I'll call the fire department!" Together we kept the burning shrubbery from setting my whole house on fire.

How did he go from pest to welcome guest so quickly? Because he had something to tell me that I instantly recognized as of urgent importance and of great value and benefit to me.

In case you had illusions to the contrary, no one is sitting around hoping and praying that they will receive your sales letter. When it arrives, it is most likely an unwelcome pest. How do you earn your welcome as a guest? By immediately saying something that is recognized by the recipient as important and valuable and beneficial.

I received a letter with this warning across the top:

WARNING: THIS LETTER IS IMPREGNATED WITH A HAZARDOUS CHEMICAL ACTIVATED IF DISCARDED UNREAD. MINUTES AFTER BEING DISCARDED, THE LETTER'S CHEMICAL WILL INTERACT WITH OTHER COMPONENTS IN YOUR WASTEBASKET AND EXPLODE INTO A GIANT GRIZZLY BEAR THAT MAY EAT YOU ALIVE. FOR YOUR OWN SAFETY AND THE SAFETY OF THOSE AROUND YOU, DO NOT DISCARD THIS LETTER UNREAD.

I clipped this top panel off, then threw the letter out unread. It's cute and funny, but there are better, more tried-and-true, honest ways of earning welcome guest status for your sales letter. Gimmicks too often fail. Saying something of genuine importance and interest to the recipient usually succeeds.

You say it with a headline.

Yes, I am well aware that advertising has headlines and letters generally do not. However, successful sales letters do. It can go above the salutation or between the salutation and the body copy. It can be typeset in big, bold type while the rest of the letter has a typewritten look. Or it can be put in a "Johnson box," a device presumably named after an inventor named Johnson, that looks like the one in the letter below:

September 12, 1990

Mr. Horace Buyer,
President
ACME Co.
123 Business Street
City, State, Zip

Dear Mr. Buyer:

****

Your headline goes here.

****

Body copy begins here and continues in normal letter format.

What your headline says and how it says it are absolutely critical. You might compare it to the door-to-door salesperson wedging a foot in the door, buying just enough time to deliver one or two sentences that will melt resistance, create interest, and elevate his or her status from annoying pest to welcome guest; you've got just about the same length of time, the same opportunity.

This book is not all about headlines, and an entire book certainly could be written about them. Instead, I've decided to give you some fill-in-the-blank headline structures that consistently and continually prove effective and successful.

FILL-IN-THE-BLANK HEADLINES WITH EXAMPLES

THEY DIDN'T THINK I COULD _____, BUT I DID.

This headline works well for many reasons, including our natural tendency to root for the underdog. We're fascinated with stories of people who overcome great obstacles and others' ridicule to achieve success. When this headline refers to something you have thought about doing, but talked yourself out of, you'll want to know if the successful person shared your doubt or fear or handicap.

Examples:

—They Laughed When I Sat Down at the Piano—But Not When I Started to Play!
—They Grinned When the Waiter Spoke to Me in French—But Their Laughter Changed to Amazement at My Reply!

WHO ELSE WANTS _____?

I like this type of headline because of its strong implication that a lot of other people know something the reader doesn't.

Examples:

—Who Else Wants a Screen-Star Figure?
—Who Else Needs an Extra Hour Every Day?

HOW _____ MADE ME _____.

This headline introduces a first-person story. People love stories and are remarkably interested in other people. This headline structure seems to work best with dramatic differences.

Examples:

—How a "Fool Stunt" Made Me a Star Salesman.
—How a Simple Idea Made Me "Plant Manager of the Year."
—How Relocating to Tennessee Saved Our Company
    One Million Dollars a Year.

ARE YOU _____?

The question headline is used to grab attention by challenging, provoking, or arousing curiosity.

Examples:

—Are You Ashamed of the Smells in Your House?
—Are You Smarter Than Your Boss?
—Are You Prepared for the Japanese Invasion of Your
    Industry?

HOW I _____.

Very much like How ____ Made Me ____, this headline introduces a first-person story. The strength of the benefit at the end, obviously, controls its success.

Examples:

—How I Raised Myself from Failure to Success in
  Selling.
—How I Retired at Age 40—With a Guaranteed Income
  for Life.
—How I Turned a Troubled Company into a Personal
  Fortune.

HOW TO _____.

This is a simple, straightforward headline structure that works with any desirable benefit. "How to" are two of the most powerful words you can use in a headline.

Examples:

—How to Collect from Social Security at any Age.
—How to Win Friends and Influence People.
—How to Improve Telemarketers' Productivity—For Just
  $19.95.

A variation on this headline is to precede it with a specific "flag": a phrase calling for the attention of a particular person.

Examples:

—For the Executive with Work Left Over Every Day: How to Delegate Without Worry.

—For Busy Doctors: How to Educate New Patients in Half the Time.

—Stock Market Investors—How to Predict Short-Term Surges and Slumps.

IF YOU ARE _____, YOU CAN _____.

This is a creative twist on the "flagging" technique shown above, a way to make the headline specific to the intended reader.

Examples:

—If You Are a Nondrinker, You Can Save 20% on Life Insurance.

—If You Are a Football Expert, You Could Win $50,000 Next Weekend.

—If Your Firm Uses "Temporaries," You Might Qualify for $1,000 in Free Services.

SECRETS OF _____.

The word "secrets" works well in headlines.

Examples:

—Secrets of a Madison Ave. Maverick—"Contrarian Advertising."

—Secrets of Four Champion Golfers.

THOUSANDS (HUNDREDS, MILLIONS) NOW _____ EVEN THOUGH THEY _____.

This is a "plural" version of the very first structure demonstrated in this collection of winning headlines.

Examples:

—Thousands Now Play Even Though They Have "Clumsy Fingers."

—Two Million People Owe Their Health to this Idea Even Though They Laughed at It.

—138,000 Members of Your Profession Receive a Check from Us Every Month Even Though They Once Threw this Letter into the Wastebasket.

WARNING: _____.

"Warning" is a powerful, attention-getting word, and can usually work for a headline tied to any sales letter using a problem-solution copy theme.

Examples:

—Warning: Two-Thirds of the Middle Managers in Your Industry Will Lose Their Jobs in the Next 36 Months.

—Warning: Your "Corporate Shield" May Be Made of Tissue Paper—9 Ways You Can Be Held Personally Liable for Your Business's Debts, Losses, or Lawsuits.

GIVE ME _____ AND I'LL _____.

This structure simplifies the gist of any sales message: a promise. It truly telegraphs your offer, and if your offer is clear and good, this may be your best strategy.

Examples:

—Give Me 5 Days and I'll Give You a Magnetic Personality.

—Give Me Just 1 Hour a Day and I'll Have You Speaking French like "Pierre" in One Month.

—Give Me a Chance to Ask Seven Questions and I'll Prove You Are Wasting a Small Fortune on Your Advertising.

_____ WAYS TO _____.

This is just the "how to" headline enhanced with an intriguing specific number.

Examples:

—101 Ways to Increase New Patient Flow.

—17 Ways to Slash Your Equipment Maintenance Costs.

Many of these example headlines are classics from very successful books, advertisements, sales letters, and brochures, obtained from a number of research sources. Some are from my own sales letters. Some were created for this book.

TIPS FOR MAILING TO EXECUTIVES AND BUSINESS OWNERS

I believe that you have to give extra concern to your letter's image when preparing mailings to executives and business owners. These people respect and generally prefer to do business with successful merchants. Remember, too, that there are intermediaries to be dealt with: receptionists and assistants who may have the option of discarding or passing along your letter. For these reasons, I suggest that you follow these guidelines.

1. Use superior quality paper and envelopes—something with a texture or watermark.
2. Avoid stuffing many advertising enclosures in the envelope. One good approach is to put your brochures, order forms, and other essential pieces inside a second sealed package, enclosed in the main envelope with your sales letter. This presents a neat, businesslike appearance and draws attention to your sales letter.
3. Incorporate prestige appeals in your sales letter with words like:

    alternative
    association
    attractive
    charter member
    exceptional
    exclusive
            il membership

ownership preferred

prominent

select

superior

uncompromising

worthwhile

yield

You can also incorporate prestige in your enclosures; plastic membership cards work well.

TIPS FOR MAILING TO THE MASS MARKET

Bear in mind the attention span of the television generation: it is very short! Without a car chase, explosion, or gunfight every 10 seconds or so, the viewer may well click the remote control unit and move on. That conditioned impatience carries over to your sales letters, as well. You've got to reach out and grab the reader where he or she lives—immediately—then do it again and again and again. One or two sentences of less-than-compelling interest, and your reader will abandon you.

Involvement devices can help you grab and hold attention. Did you ever notice how Publishers Clearinghouse has you tearing out little stamps and pasting them onto the order card? Rub-off cards, tokens, stickers, and similar devices get the reader involved with the mailing.

You should also remember that color is virtually essential in consumer mailings. A number of bright, differently colored pieces are beneficial—as is color photography.

TIPS FOR MAILINGS TO SELL PRODUCTS DIRECTLY

When you want the reader to make a decision to buy this item now—not commit to some intangible service or complicated agreement—you must follow several important guidelines:

1. Use testimonials from happy users of the product; these will do more than anything else to increase sales.
2. Remember that photographs outperform drawings and illustrations.
3. Prove that the product is easy to use. This may be done with copy, photographs, or testimonials—but it must be done!

TIPS FOR MAILINGS TO SELL PROFESSIONAL SERVICES

Credibility is critical here. Descriptive items of fact (such as number of years in business, number of clients served, sample client lists, and so on) can all be of tremendous value.

Consider offering a free initial consultation or a free package of informative literature; this may break down barriers of skepticism and mistrust. Answer the question: why should the reader bother? Similarly, you should work at making the intangible benefits of your product tangible. This can be accomplished with before/after photographs, slice-of-life stories, case histories, or other examples. Demonstrate the value!

7

BEAT THE
PRICE BUGABOO

Although any good sales pro will admit that price is very rarely the determining factor in a buying decision, that same pro will tell you that, mishandled, price can put the brakes on a sale before it even gets going.

The sales-letter writer has to decide, before actually writing the letter, how to present price and what strategies to use in minimizing the impact of price. Certainly, if price is a key issue in your business, you'll want to minimize it to whatever degree possible in the mind of your letter recipient. Here, then, are the best price minimizers I know.

COMPARE APPLES TO ORANGES

There's no law that says you have to stick with logical, apples-to-apples comparisons. You are much better off with a comparison that confuses the price issue.

In a publishing/mail-order company I ran for five years, we sold specialized, high-priced audiocassette courses to dentists and chiropractors. The going price for a spoken-word, business-oriented audiocassette was—and still is—about $10. Most of the companies in this business price a six-cassette album at $49.95 to $69.95—$8.33 to $11.66 a tape. Our single programs, however, averaged out to at least $16.58 and as much as $23.00 per tape. The last thing we wanted to do was compare the prices of our apples and their apples! Instead, we compared the prices of our cassette programs to the costs of attending the seminars on which the tapes were based. For example: ". . . to attend the Practice Promotion Seminar just one time would cost you at least $195 as an enrollment fee, plus travel, lodging overnight, and the time away from your practice or your family—certainly several hundred dollars or more. But when you get this same important information in cassette form, you can listen and learn at your convenience, share with associates and staff members, and pay only $95."

I continue to use this very same cassettes-to-seminars, apples-to-oranges comparison today, in sales letter after sales letter, for over a dozen different clients in the publishing industry, proving the reliability of the strategy. Whatever your product, service, or offer, you need to look for a way to make easy, direct-price comparison difficult.

SELL BULK

People do equate value with bulk. One of the very first sales letters for an offer of books was for the Harvard Classics, and it proudly proclaimed its bulk: "Dr. Elliott's Five-Foot Shelf of Books." I shamelessly copied this idea for a client, with this line: "These three information-packed books weigh over thirteen pounds and cost nearly twenty dollars just to ship to your door!"

One of my clients, a Platinum-level Kennedy Inner Circle Member, very recently emphasized this idea in one of his sales letters, saying: ". . . and you'd better go down to Wal-Mart and buy the biggest bookshelf you can buy, for the huge truckload of moneymaking information in books, manuals, and courses that I'm going to give you, free, when . . ."

If you are selling an information product like books, cassettes, or subscriptions, remember that one way to convey bulk is with a list of the 1,001 (or some other huge, specific number) pieces of information contained in your product. You'll see the leaders in this field, like Boardroom Reports and Rodale Press do this repeatedly.

If you are selling some other type of product, the same principle applies. Just for example, if we were writing a sales letter for an ordinary apple, instead of just saying that "an apple a day keeps the doctor away," we might list every vitamin and mineral provided by the apple, then list every health benefit delivered by each of those vitamins and minerals. We might then show the huge bulk of other foods you'd have to consume to get those same nutrients and benefits—all to turn that little apple into a huge "bulk" of benefits and value.

DISCUSS THE PRICE PAID TO DEVELOP THE OFFER

Is this relevant to the consumer? Maybe not, but that doesn't prevent you from making it relevant.

Consider the difference between these two ways of telling you about a piece of automated industrial equipment:

VERSION #1:

It automatically selects the right amount of material, fills the bag, seals it, and stacks it in the carton. It gets it right every time. And it is an extraordinarily durable system, good for tens of thousands of repetitions without needing maintenance.

VERSION #2:

Our company recruited a brain trust of eight of the very best, most knowledgeable robotics engineers in industry today to design this system. No expense was spared in obtaining the services of these experts. The prototype system was run over six months of laboratory tests at a cost of over one million dollars before ever being placed in an actual working environment. In the ultimate test, we put it through 15,000 repetitions, and it performed perfectly and never needed even a minute of downtime for maintenance. You can count on this system to select the right amount of material every time, fill the bag, seal it, and stack it in the carton without error. With over three million dollars' worth of research and quality control backing you up, you'll finally have at least one piece of equipment working for you that is as reliable as God's sunrise.

Both copy versions describe the same machine and the exact same benefits. But the second version builds value.

MAKE THE PARTS WORTH MORE
THAN THE WHOLE

Have you ever seen the "pitchmen" at the state or county fair, with crowds gathered around them, selling things like slicer-dicers, sets of kitchen knives, or similar gadgets? These people are artistic masters at building high perceived value for each little doodad, each attachment, each part, so that when it's all added up it is much, much more than the price of the whole unit. The "value overage" in such presentations is overwhelming. This same strategy works in more sophisticated settings, too.

Consider this example:

The typical doctor saves thousands of dollars with our Full-Service System Concept for practice promotion and management. Consider the value of everything you get as a System Client:

6 SEMINARS DURING THE 24-MONTH CONTRACT

Each 2-Day Seminar focuses on a different aspect of practice success: Advertising, Referrals, Money Management, and much more. Each Seminar features appropriate expert guest lecturers as well as our Team Trainers. If you sought out individually offered seminars covering these same topic areas, you would pay at least $195 to as much as $395 for each one. So this is at least a $1200 value.

THE 24-MONTH MARKETING KIT

24 newspaper ads, 24 different patient newsletters, 24 different seasonal referral stimulation letter campaigns, 24 different in-office hand-outs . . . all designed by our own advertising experts, an advisory group of 10 successful doctors, and Dr. Bill Whosis himself. We've priced this—the typical ad agency would charge over $10,000 to create all this for you from scratch! Even if you did it yourself, and just hired freelancers to do the typesetting,

illustrations, and layout work, you'd spend at least $3,000, probably more.

TAPE-OF-THE-MONTH CLUB

Each month you'll receive a new Audiocassette, for your own use, and a new Videocassette with four Staff Meeting Starter Sessions on it. Just at prevailing prices for general-interest audio and video materials, this is nearly a $1,000 value. Of course, this specialized practice building information is worth much more!

If you add this all up, you've got at least $5,200 in "hard value," in reality, a lot more—but your entire 24-Month Fee is only $3,895! And that's not all! When you join us within the next 60 days . . . before the end of this calendar year . . . you receive three very special, valuable bonus gifts and services ABSOLUTELY FREE!

First, a monthly review of your statistics and finances by our team of accountants, financial planners and doctors, followed by a one-page Report of Findings and Recommendations. Second, our famous "How to Build Community Prominence" Self-Study Course with 6 audio tapes, 1 video tape and a 200-page Manual . . . including interviews with seven very successful doctors from different parts of the country about their public relations successes. And, three, an opportunity to compete in our "Most Improved Doctor of the Year" competition, for an expense-paid Hawaiian vacation and exciting runner-up prizes.

CONCEAL THE PRICE

This is a relatively new strategy being used in print ads, sales letters, even television commercials for a variety of consumer-product, book, and subscription offers. These marketers present prices like this: "Just three small monthly installments of $11.95 charged to your credit card."

While this has taken hold as a "norm" only in the past handful of years for the entire direct-response industry, the approach is not really much of an innovation; the automobile industry has been using it for some time. I just got a sales letter from a local Cadillac dealership about its annual used car sale; the letter included an 8½-by-11-inch list of all the cars, arranged by brand, model, color, options, and stock number. The cars were grouped into "payment categories"—one list at $99 per month, one at $149 per month, another at $199 per month.

THREE LETTER FORMULAS THAT LET YOU TRANSCEND PRICE QUESTIONS

Now let's look at three of the most effective copywriting formulas you can use to overcome a reader's hesitation on the issue of price (and on many other issues as well). These formulas relate to the price question because they get the reader to focus on something other than how much money he is going to spend—and isn't that your objective?

The formulas are easy to understand, adaptable to many business situations, and—most important—they work.

FORMULA #1
PROBLEM-AGITATION-SOLUTION

When you understand that people are more likely to act to avoid pain than to get gain, you'll understand how incredibly powerful this first formula is. I have used this basic formula to structure super-effective sales presentations for live salespeople in every imaginable business, from security systems to skin-care products. I've used it for over 136 different industries, and not only for sales letters, but also for salespeople. It may be *the* most reliable sales formula ever invented.

The first step is to define the customer's problem. You may be writing about a problem they know they have or about a problem they don't know they have—it matters very little, because a good sales letter avoids assuming knowledge on the part of the recipient. So the letter sets forth the problem in clear, straightforward terms. You need to say here only enough to elicit agreement. For a letter promoting a tax-strategies course for small business owners, this part of the letter can be very brief:

> You, the small business owner, are already the government's #1 tax target. Every time you look at your mail, there's another tax form demanding your attention and your money. Now you will also pay the highest price for the new tax reform—unless you discover a few secrets normally used only by "the big guys" to fight back!

If you're presenting a more complex problem, you may need to say a great deal more and add proof to your premise. I had a client I wrote a number of sales letters for some years ago who was a consultant on employee and deliveryman theft in retail businesses. Because most retailers (incorrectly and stubbornly) believe that their theft problems are with shoplifters rather than their own employees, I had to take as much as half the letter to demonstrate with facts, statistics, case examples, and other credible information that their real problem was internal.

Once the problem is established, clearly and factually, it's time to inject emotion. This second step is agitation. That means we stir up the letter recipients' emotional responses to the problem. We tap their anger, resentment, guilt, embarrassment, fear—any and every applicable negative emotion. We want to whip them into a fervor! We want to make the problem larger than life, worse than death.

My sales-trainer friend, the famous (late) Cavett Robert, said to sell life insurance or cemetery plots, you have to make your customer see the hearse backed up to the door. That may sound a little grisly, but it's true.

Here's agitation copy from a sales letter for a very ordinary product: shoes.

> . . . but if you insist on just wearing any old pair of ordinary shoes, here's what you have to look forward to in your so-called golden years: fallen arches . . . intense lower back pain . . . extraordinary discomfort in golf or tennis shoes . . . even pain from just walking around a shopping mall! You'll be asking your friends to slow down so you can keep up. You'll be futilely soaking your feet at night like some old fuddy-duddy. You may even need pain pills just to get to sleep.

And here's agitation copy from one of the sales letters sent to CEOs of grocery-store chains by my theft-control expert:

> The next time you look out the big picture window of your home at your beautiful, manicured lawn, think about this: a client of mine, the owner of 16 supermarkets, told me he was doing just that—looking happily out his window across his lawn at the half-million-dollar home diagonally across the street where his new neighbors were moving in. Imagine his shock when he realized his new neighbor was the driver of the soft-drink delivery truck

that serviced his supermarkets! Yes, that deliveryman was paying for his half-million-dollar home with money from the goods he had stolen from my client's supermarkets!

You worked hard to build up your business. The employees and vendors stealing from you have no capital investment in stores, no bank loans to worry about, no tax forms to fill out. You've earned your success and they're stealing it from you, right under your nose! And if you refuse to see it, you are "the emperor with no clothes." In fact, they're laughing at you, right now, behind your back. I know. I was one of them. Long before I became a security consultant, I was a deliveryman-thief! I conspired with other deliverymen just like the ones who service your stores. I conspired with employees just like the ones working in your stores. And together we stole and stole and stole some more.

If you were the owner of a chain of stores, would that rattle your cage a little? (By the way, please note that everything I wrote about the expert—whose signature appeared on the above letter—was true.)

After you've clearly stated the problem, and after you've created tremendous agitation about the problem, you should have readers mentally wringing their hands, pacing the room, saying: "This has got to stop! I've got to do something about this! What can I do about this? If only there were an answer!" And that's right where you want them!

It's at that point, that crucial moment, that you whip out the solution. The third step is to unveil the solution, the answer—your product or services, and the accompanying benefits.

Here's an example of a complete sales letter using this formula:

Dear Computer Hater,

DO YOU HATE YOUR COMPUTER?

DO YOU OWN A COMPUTER THAT WON'T DO WHAT YOU TELL IT TO DO?

ARE YOU AFRAID TO BUY A COMPUTER— EVEN THOUGH YOU KNOW YOU NEED ONE?

ARE YOU CONFUSED BY COMPUTER-BABBLE?

In a recent survey taken by the Small Business Research Institute, over 74% of the small business owners who had purchased computers in the past 12 months <u>felt they had been "ripped off"</u> . . . lied to about what the computers would do for them; how easy they were to use; or the help and support available. Over 30% said their costly computers were now being used as typewriters or, worse, sitting in a corner gathering dust.

If you're in this group of frustrated, disappointed computer owners, you've literally <u>flushed thousands, maybe tens of thousands of dollars right down the toilet!!!</u> Is that how a savvy businessperson behaves? Of course not!

If you're afraid to "computerize" because of these problems— well, do successful businesspeople live in fear? Of course not.

We have the solution you need.

We're "PC SOLUTIONS," and here's what we'll do for you:

1. We will always talk with you in plain English. No computer-babble.

2. We will objectively analyze your needs "from scratch." We'll tell you what a computer system will and will not do for you.

3. If you already have computer equipment and software, we will:

   A. Evaluate it and help you understand it—quickly
   B. Make it work for you, if possible
   C. Teach your people how to use it
   D. If it's "wrong" for you, we'll do battle with whoever sold it to you to get it traded in, replaced or repaired
   E. If necessary, we'll modify it or add to it at the lowest cost possible

4. If you haven't purchased computers yet, we'll guide you in doing so . . . picking the right equipment and software for your needs. We do NOT sell computers or software. We're on your side!

Why suffer with unproductive computers, unhappy staff, anger, frustration? Call PC-SOLUTIONS today for a FREE, NO-OBLIGATION 30-MINUTE CONSULTATION.

1-800-DISKJOY

FORMULA #2
FORTUNE TELLING

Our fascination with those who predict the future never ends. One very savvy public relations agent told me: "The two keys to unlimited media attention and publicity are being predictive and being provocative." Who's going to win the Super Bowl this year? What will the stock market do next? When will the earthquake occur? What will happen in the new millennium? And on and on and on.

John Naisbitt rose from obscurity to celebrity as a best-selling author, business guru, highly paid lecturer, consultant, and social commentator, all thanks to his predictive book

Megatrends. Another author, Doug Casey, created similar prominence for himself with his predictive book *Crisis Investing.* One of the sales letters for his newsletter does an outstanding job of utilizing this predictive posture to motivate readership of the sales letter itself and to sell the subscription. This sales letter masterfully manipulates both fear of and fascination with the future.

What lies ahead in your industry? For your customers or clients? How can you help them prepare now for the future? Is there a "clear and present danger" you can help them protect against? Is there a budding opportunity you can help them take advantage of? Is there an exciting new trend they can attach themselves to?

When you bring the future to the present, as this Doug Casey letter did, you fascinate your readers!

By the way, this strategy was widely used and very visible in promoting all sorts of "Y2K" related products, from gas generators to freeze-dried food supplies to gold coins, as the clock ticked toward January 1, 2000. In the years leading up to this date, companies selling everything from computer software and insurance to freeze-dried food and bottled water, religious organizations, authors, and publishers all profited enormously by issuing dire predictions of what could or might happen. The same kind of material you see here in this *Crisis Investing* piece from back in 1987 was recycled and used in 1999, 12 years later.

This is as good a time as any to call your attention to that recurring theme: good, solid, time-tested sales/sales letter strategies do not wear out or become obsolete. What worked in a sales letter in 1950 will still work in 2050, with only slight language modification.

ENCLOSED:
Doug Casey's new investment predictions for 1987

■ We are already in the beginning phases of the next Great Depression—which promises to be much worse than the last one! But this economic upheaval will provide spectacular opportunities—*profits of 500% to 1000%*—for shrewd investors *(see page 1).*

■ A surprising list of global investment "hot spots" *(see page 5).*

■ 3 best opportunities to make your million(s) in the second half of the '80s *(see page 3 inside).*

■ Escalating problems in South Africa will trigger a price explosion in certain raw materials *(see page 1).*

■ Suicide terrorists will soon be able to hold entire cities hostage—with undetectable nuclear mini-bombs. *Primary targets*: Wall Street, Silicon Valley and other key economic centers *(see page 4 inside).*

■ A financial accident will spark the greatest bank panic since the Great Depression. *(11 of today's unsafest big financial institutions are named on page 4 inside)*

■ Higher interest rates will return. Bonds will be mauled *(see page 4).*

■ Special recommendation concerning T-bills *(see page 4 inside).*

■ **PLUS,** *a unique opportunity to get rich as a "white-collar" farmer. You could actually have the potential to run a portfolio of $10,000 into $150,000 within the next two years (see page 6 inside).*

Please turn over to page 1 for more details...

INVESTING IN CRISIS
P.O. Box 1464
Alexandria, VA 22313

BULK RATE
U.S. POSTAGE

402187

DAN S KENNEDY
PHOENIX, AZ 85020

Reprinted courtesy of Agora Publishing Co., Baltimore, Maryland.

FORMULA #3
WINNERS AND LOSERS

Very early in my selling career, I was taught a "pitch" that reads/ sounds something like this:

> Take any hundred people at the start of their working careers and follow them for 40 years until they reach retirement age, and here's what you'll find, according to the Social Security Administration: only 1 will be wealthy; 4 will be financially secure; 5 will continue working, not because they want to but because they have to; 36 will be dead; and 54 will be dead broke—dependent on their meager Social Security checks, relatives, friends, even charity for a minimum standard of living. That's 5% successful, 95% unsuccessful.

That same basic comparison has been used to sell everything from life insurance and investments to real-estate-buying schemes and Amway distributorships. I have used it face-to-face, speaking from the platform and in print, thousands and thousands of times. It quickly gains attention, opens minds, and makes people think. Then, whatever it is you are selling is presented as the path to joining the 5% group, the big difference between the winners and the losers.

The reason I was taught this material and the reason it is used so widely, repetitively, and continuously is that it works. People understand it. It creates fear—fear of being in the 95% group. It creates motivation—motivation to be in the 5% group.

The *Wall Street Journal* has used variations of this theme in many of its sales letters over the years. One of its most successful sales letters tells the story of two college graduates—one successful, one not, with the difference being that one subscribes to the *Journal*.

Here's an example of the formula from a sales letter I wrote for a lawn and garden store back in the early 1970s:

Last spring, two neighbors reseeded their lawns. Now it's June. One has a beautiful, lush, thick green lawn. As perfect as the best golf course in the country. A lawn to be proud of.

His neighbor, though, has a different lawn. With little brown patches. Uneven texture. Crabgrass and weeds fighting for territory.

What made the difference?

The letter goes on to tout the virtues of "lawn care counseling" from the store's owners and a particular line of lawn care products and fertilizers. It will work just as well today (in the right geographic areas—the 'burbs) as it did almost 20 years ago. In fact, in 1998, I recycled it for a landscaping company's franchisees, and several have reported phenomenal results.

These three formulas can be used separately or combined in a single sales letter. At least one of them and probably all of them can work for your business.

Step

8

REVIEW WINNING COPYWRITING TECHNIQUES AND TACTICS

I once flew across the country seated next to a grizzled, old-time direct-sales pro who told me about getting started during the tail-end of the Depression, selling vacuum cleaners door to door. When the sales manager hired this fellow, he gave him a giant looseleaf notebook of 299 "sales techniques" to use in getting past the front door, demonstrating the vacuum, and closing the sale. He had to memorize and be tested on his knowledge of those techniques before going out into the field.

"How many of the two hundred and ninety-nine did you wind up using?" I asked him.

"Oh, I tried 'em all," he said, "but after thirty days in the trenches I was down to using the three or four that worked."

I've had similar experiences with copywriting. Early in my career, I assembled a reference library of literally h books about advertising, marketing, direct response, direct mail, mail order, and copywriting, each full of dozens of different techniques. I suppose I've tried hundreds of them. And, over the years, I've narrowed it down to a handful that work consistently and almost universally. So, consider this an enormously valuable shortcut. If you want to experiment I guess that's fine, but if you simply want to be effective and efficient, then you can stick with these few formulas, and you can probably take care of all your sales letter needs for years to come just with these few formulas.

Here they are.

TECHNIQUE #1
INTIMIDATION

In person-to-person, professional selling, I very quickly learned the value of intimidation, and I consider Robert Ringer's bestselling book *Winning Through Intimidation* to be one of the most useful business books I've ever read. From that book and my own experiences, I learned that the hardest deal to make is the one you desperately need or really, really want to make. Somehow, the other person always senses that, and it scares him or her away. On the other hand, the easiest deals to close occur when you feel that you don't need them and really don't much care whether they come to fruition or not. This is called "taking a position," and it applies equally well to selling in print.

Here are some interesting ways to "take a position."

1. Limited Number Available

Mints, sellers of collectibles, and rare coin dealers use this strategy with great effectiveness, but it's certainly not limited to them. Many times I've used copy like this connected to a limited-quantity offer:

> . . . if your response is received after our supply is exhausted, it will not be accepted and your check will be returned uncashed.

This is intimidating!

2. Most Will Buy

This technique relies on what is sometimes called the "bandwagon effect," creating the idea that a huge trend has developed, everybody is getting involved, and anyone who passes it up is, quite simply, an idiot. Here's an example of this kind of copy:

> . . . thousands have joined in the last 30 days. Only a small number of people have received this invitation, and we fully expect most of them to take immediate advantage of this amazing discount—so if our phone lines are busy when you call, please be patient and keep trying. We have added extra customer-service people to handle everybody's calls as rapidly as possible.

3. You Will Buy Only If . . .

In a way, this is the opposite of #2—a challenge to the reader's ego and pride. For example:

> . . . of course it takes a very special individual to appreciate the value of authentic Cromwell Crystal fully. Even though we've been very selective in choosing the people to

receive this invitation, we also realize that only about 5 out of every 100 will respond.

4. You *Can* Buy Only If . . .

This is an interesting tactic. I have a client who markets expensive (i.e., $5000 and up) home-study courses on business and self-improvement. At various times, he has required prospective purchasers to listen to seven hours of introductory material and sign an official-looking affidavit attesting that they had done so before they were permitted to buy. Another client, a trade school, requires prospective students to furnish letters of reference.

A letter from a franchisor used the tactic this way:

> We are very particular about the people we select as business associates, so you're welcome to write in or call for the free information kit, but don't get your hopes up just yet! Read everything thoroughly. Then, if you think you can qualify, you'll have to complete a detailed questionnaire, which will be reviewed by our Advisory Committee. Only if you are approved at that stage will you be invited to come to the Home Office for a personal interview.

5. Only Some Can Qualify . . .

This is a variation on #4. American Express has used this tactic for years in connection with its cards, particularly its Gold Card. It appeals to the person's desire to be part of an elite group, for approval and recognition.

6. Strong Credibility Copy

You can intimidate away a reader's doubts and fears with a super-strong explanation of your credibility.

For example:

> In 10 years, the American Back School has trained over 2 million individuals and 140,000 trainers and practitioners, including many for *Fortune* 500 corporations and the United States Armed Forces.

TECHNIQUE #2
DEMONSTRATE ROI

ROI is return on investment. In business-to-business sales letters, it's very important to talk about, promise, and, if possible, demonstrate. Even when marketing to consumers, it can be helpful to show that the proposed purchase actually costs nothing, thanks to the savings or profit it produces.

Demonstrating ROI puts you in the position of "selling money at a discount." Imagine having this job to do: stand in front of a crowd and offer as many $1000 bills as anyone would like to buy—for $50 each. To start with, most people have never seen a $1000 bill and would assume you were a counterfeiter, so you'd need experts there to attest to the authenticity of the product. Then you'd need to make it easy to buy, maybe by accepting Visa or MasterCard. And so on. But certainly if you did convince them that the bills were real and the offer was legitimate, you'd have no trouble unloading as much product as you wanted! Well, that's what you can do when you demonstrate ROI.

ROI can be presented in terms of dollars to be made. For example, this copy:

> Over 1000 doctors reported specific increases in their incomes last year as a result of our course. Many reported net gains of $10,000 to $25,000. Once it's been repeated 1000 times, it's no accident—it's a proven system you can use, too. Its cost? Just $199. So even a $1000 income increase represents a 500% return on your investment!

ROI can also be presented in terms of dollars to be saved. For example, this copy:

> If you paid more than $300 in federal taxes last year, I guarantee this newsletter will be worth at least $150 to you—and it costs only $29.95! That's a 500% return on investment, guaranteed.

It sometimes pays to exaggerate your ROI promise, then bring the reader back down with copy like this:

> . . . and even if I'm only half right, you'll still pocket over $ . . . .

This creates a feeling of reasonableness, conservatism, even objectivity—all reassuring to the reader.

TECHNIQUE #3
EGO APPEALS

If everything bought in America in order to "keep up with the Joneses" were laid end to end, we'd probably have a durable-goods bridge reaching at least from here to Mars. Yes, ego is alive and well. When a product, a service, an association with a certain company, or any offer is convincingly portrayed as a status symbol, you've got the basis of a good sales letter.

There are many practical reasons for owning a fax machine. I rank it as one of the all-time best pieces of office equipment ever developed. But in talking with a marketer of such machines, very early in the game—when fax machines were still "new," I realized that my ego, just as much as the convenience of the machine, was a motivating factor in my decision to purchase. The marketer and I discussed this, and came up with the following copy:

WHAT EXCUSE DO YOU MAKE WHEN ASKED FOR YOUR FAX NUMBER— AND YOU HAVEN'T GOT ONE?

Can you afford to appear "behind the times" to your clients, customers, vendors, and associates? Or is it important to you to be perceived as successful, savvy, in tune with the trends leading the American business scene?

Well, that "pitch" dates back to 1991. These days, virtually every office and many homes have fax machines. But I hope you recognized the universal nature of that "pitch." These days, it is being used to sell cellular phones and Internet sites. And whatever the next, new technology is that comes along, it too can and will be sold at some point based on Ego Appeal. Again, this is not limited to tech products. You'll see it used, for example, to sell the newest innovations in golf clubs or tennis rackets, automobiles— right now, this is the basis for Cadillac's TV commercials emphasizing its "Northstar System."

TECHNIQUE #4
STRONG GUARANTEE

Some direct marketing "authorities" have recently been pontificating about guarantees being out-of-date and ineffective with today's supposedly more sophisticated consumers. However, practical experience continues to prove that, one, a guarantee boosts response, and two, the better the guarantee, the better the response.

In fact, some research I've seen does indicate a heightened, harsher skepticism on the part of today's consumers. This is not just a consumer trend, but a societal one, largely supported by the repetitive failures of people we once looked up to: political leaders, ministers, and pro athletes. We have been in a "trust depression" and "skepticism growth phase" since President Nixon's abrupt departure from the presidency. People like Oliver North, Jim and Tammy Bakker, Jimmy Swaggart, and Pete Rose didn't help matters much. Bill and Hillary et al. have poured gasoline on the cynicism fire. My conviction, though, is that this heightened consumer skepticism calls for better and stronger guarantees—not the abandonment of the guarantee.

One of the greatest business success stories of our time in consumer marketing has been built on this foundation: "fresh, hot pizza delivered in 30 minutes or less, guaranteed." Similarly, one of the greatest business-to-business marketing success stories of our time was built with the slogan "absolutely, positively overnight."

Here are the best ways to use a guarantee in your sales letters.

1. Basic Money-Back Guarantee

This is the simple, basic approach: if, for any reason, you are not fully satisfied with your purchase, return it for a full refund. I like to see this basic guarantee creatively embellished with livelier wording. You might say "delighted" or "thrilled" or even use fancier language, rather than "satisfied." You could opt for a folksier approach: ". . . return the widget for a full refund—no hassles, no hard feelings."

If it's unusual for a guarantee to be offered in your type of business, don't be bashful about saying so. For example: "Our guarantee is doubly important when you realize that no other widget maker offers one!"

2. Refund and Keep the Premium

You can strengthen your guarantee by linking it with a premium (free bonus gift). Example: "If you're not thrilled with your subscription, you may cancel, receive a full refund, and still keep the leatherbound appointment diary free, with our compliments! That's how absolutely certain we are that you will find tremendous value in every issue of . . ."

3. Redundancy

Another way to strengthen the presentation of your guarantee is to be deliberately redundant. Say the same thing twice or even three times! For example: "Receive a full 100% refund of every penny you paid."

4. Free Trial Offer

You can give your guarantee a different twist by presenting it as a free trial offer. Example: "You take no risk with our Free Trial Offer! If you're not happy with the Rocket-Z Weed Whacker, just return it anytime within 90 days for a full refund."

5. Make the Guarantee the Primary Focus of the Offer

You can sometimes increase the effectiveness of your entire sales letter by making the guarantee the featured item. The publisher of a financial newsletter achieved his greatest success when he started his sales letter this way:

> Income tax savings guaranteed—or your money back! If, in the first three issues of my newsletter, you haven't found ways to decrease your taxes . . .

By the way, the use of a guarantee need not be limited to product offers. Many travel agents guarantee their customers the lowest available fares. Copier companies guarantee their equipment will not exceed a specified amount of downtime. Restaurants guarantee lunch served in 15 minutes. With a little imagination and a genuine commitment to excellence, you can find a way to bring a guarantee into your marketing arsenal.

Now let me give you an advanced technique. This requires several things: first, brass balls; second, a real understanding of the prospects and how they'll behave; and third, a strong sales message you're certain will be of significant interest to the recipients of the sales letter. The daring strategy is to guarantee the letter. I actually use this strategy a lot, for myself and for clients. Often, we'll offer $10, $20, or $50 if the recipient reads the entire sales letter and feels his time has been wasted. An actual sample of this is on the next page, from a very recent mailing I did for a seminar. In this case, I paid out less than $200 from mailing to nearly 4000 prospects, but I brought in over $100,000 in profits. And we know from "split-testing" a number of times that the addition of the "this letter is guaranteed" does increase readership and response.

This Free Information Package Is Guaranteed

How can something sent to you free be guaranteed? Here's my promise: if you read the attached, admittedly lengthy letter about your speaking business and listen to the enclosed audio cassettes and watch the enclosed video, and you honestly feel I've wasted your time, just jot me a note to that effect on the back of this certificate and I'll either pay you $25.00 or donate $50.00 to Habitat For Humanity, your choice.

Since I'm sending out about 2,000 of these packages, that puts me on the hook for $100,000.00. That's okay, I can afford it. But I'm betting on your integrity as a professional colleague, and I'm betting on the fact that, even if you decide to say "no" to the offer extended to you in this information, at the very least you'll have to admit to picking up a valuable marketing idea or two you can use in your business, so this can't be a waste of time. Anyway, it's up to you. With my Guarantee, you can't lose by paying attention to this.

Sincerely,

Dan S. Kennedy

NOTE: PLEASE (1) LISTEN TO THE "SPILL THE BEANS" AUDIO TAPE FIRST THEN (2) WATCH THE VIDEO, THEN (3) READ THE LETTER, THEN (4) LISTEN TO THE "$25,000.00 A DAY" TAPE LAST. IT IS VERY IMPORTANT TO (AT LEAST) HEAR THE "SPILL THE BEANS TAPE" BEFORE READING THE LETTER.

In a somewhat similar fashion, I have a client in the financial services and asset protection business who sends out 100 of his sales letters on the first day of each month, targeting only owners or CEOs of corporations in his city, known to have personal net worths exceeding $5 million. In his sales letter, he suggests that in just 19 minutes of conversation, he can reveal a dangerous "hole" in their financial fortresses or an opportunity to save on their income taxes that their current CPA, lawyer, or other advisors have not called to their attention. If he fails, he'll pay them $250 or donate $500 to the charity of their choice. With this courageous approach, he usually secures 10 to 15 appointments per 100 letters mailed (a 10% to 15% response), converts 2 to 3 of the 10 or 15 into new clients, with an average first year value per client of $10,000 or more.

WRITE THE FIRST DRAFT

This chapter is short because its idea is a simple one. Put what you've learned so far to work!

Up until now, the steps of the system have put you through a great deal of preparatory work. Now you can start doing what you wanted to do in the first place—write!

You can now write a first draft. Don't edit as you go. Don't worry about length, grammar, or anything else—just write.

I usually wind up with a first draft two, even three times the length my letter ultimately winds up, but I prefer to get every possible persuasive idea onto the table and face the editing challenge later. I think this is, by far, the easiest of the many writing approaches I've seen copywriters use.

Drop your inhibitions, sharpen your pencil, and see what happens!

10

REWRITE FOR STRATEGY

You've written your first draft; it's probably too long. Now comes the rewrite stage. For many writers, this is the beginning of the process whereby one whittles away at a project until it contains a single clear, concise message.

But there is more to rewriting than cutting—and there are many sales letters that work despite (and perhaps because of!) a lot of text. In this chapter, we'll look at the "strategic" rewrites you should make to increase reader response to your letter.

SECRETS OF SUCCESSFUL LONG COPYWRITING

"Who's going to read all that copy?" I can't tell you how many times I've been asked that question by a shocked, incredulous client staring at a sales letter that appeared to resemble a novel more closely than a note.

The answer is: those people most likely to respond.

Most research shows that the vast majority of readers never go beyond a quick glance at an advertisement, and the same is true about most sales letters. Even with excellent list selection, you'll still be sending your sales letters to a great many people who give them only a passing glance as they toss them into their wastebaskets. These people just are not interested in your product or service; they are not interested in *anything* at the moment except clearing their desks; they can't read, won't read, or for any number of other reasons are 100% resistant to your message. Worrying about whether this majority will read one page, half a page, or any other given quantity of copy is a foolish exercise—who cares? Trying to trick or manipulate these people into reading is extraordinarily difficult and of questionable value. Shortening your copy to a length everybody will read is counterproductive. Instead, we need to focus our energies on the relative minority of the letter recipients who will be interested in the message. In other words, write for the buyer, not the nonbuyer.

Real prospects are hungry for information—so says Ogilvy and Mather, one of the largest and most astutely run ad agencies in the world.

According to Ogilvy and Mather, research indicates that industrial ads with extensive text actually are read more thoroughly than shorter-copy pieces. Readership drops precipitously up to about 50 words; it drops much less between 50 and 500 words.

Early in my copywriting career, this kind of information inspired me to use long sales letters, usually 4 to as many as 16 pages. Rather than concern myself with the length of my letters, I chose to concentrate on telling seriously interested, qualified prospects everything they might possibly need to know to respond positively. If that required 16 pages, then 16 pages it was!

I have followed this principle for over 20 years and am unwaveringly convinced of its validity. In some cases, we have started a campaign with a one- or two-page letter and gotten encouraging results; added a page or two and gotten better results; then added another page or two and gotten even better results!

STRATEGIC REWRITING

Following are some guidelines that have proven successful for developing your sales letter at this stage.

Write and Rewrite Without Restraint

Have you ever wondered how there's just enough news each day to fit perfectly on the front page of the newspaper? Obviously, there isn't; articles are continued on subsequent pages, and some stories receive coverage for consecutive days, even weeks. Still, many reporters do write under editor-imposed length limits. So, to some degree, all the news that fits—be it 15 inches of needed column text or no more than 300 words—gets printed.

This is no way to sell. If you were a sales manager, would you send your representatives out into the field with the instruction, "Whatever you do, don't say more than 300 words!" I don't think so. Let's remember that a sales letter is a sales presentation in print.

It bears repeating: do not write to fit a predetermined format or number of pages. Write to tell your story successfully.

Frustrate the English Teachers

My sales letters make lots of English teachers unhappy. They cringe and moan and groan. I've even occasionally received "critiques" from these dedicated grammarians. There's good reason for this: successful sales letters read much more like we talk than the way we're supposed to write. They use conversational English and popular slang. They often employ choppy sentences frowned on by style books: "It's a fact. It's guaranteed. It's proven. Under the intense heat and burning sun of the Salt Flats."

Schoolbook grammar is irrelevant in the sales letter. Instead, use every weapon in your arsenal—odd punctuation and phrasing, nonsentences, one-word exclamations, buzzwords—to push and prod and pull the reader along, and to create momentum and excitement.

Have you ever been around a young kid, maybe 10 or 12 years old, very excitedly telling you about some toy he or she wants, some place the kid wants to go, or something he or she wants to do? They talk so fast they stumble and stutter, rushing on without taking a breath. They never complete a sentence. And this enthusiasm is infectious. Inject that kind of action into your sales letter and you'll have a winner. Oh, and by the way—when you go to the bank to deposit all the profits your sales letter produced, nobody will ask whether you dangled a participle or split an infinitive while you were making the money.

Increase Readership with the Double Readership Path

We can divide our recipients into two personality extremes: the impulsive and the analytical. While most sales letters appeal to one extreme at the expense of the other due to the personality of the writer, we can appeal to both extremes in the same letter. The *analytical* prospect is a logical, methodical person. If they are going to buy a new car, for example, they'll make a research project out of it. The *impulsive* prospect, on the other hand, buys a new car because it's red! It's obvious that these people should be addressed differently.

The impulsive one will rarely read long copy, and, if they do, they'll read it only after heightening their interest by first somehow skimming the letter. For them, you need to "telegraph" your offer and its benefits. They want to skim and get the gist of your offer very quickly. This is an impatient person, one for whom you need to create an impulsive readership path through your letter that consists of big, bold headlines and subheads; photos with captions; and boxed, circled, or highlighted short paragraphs. While reading just those things, while running along that path, your impulsive reader needs to get enough information to respond.

Frequently, after skimming, the impulsive prospect will slow down and read and consider the entire long sales letter. This is our goal.

For the analytical prospect, we can provide a more complete readership path. The Impulsive Path becomes just the signposts along the Analytical Path. The analytical prospects will read long copy—in fact, they almost require it! They want lots of facts, figures, statistics, charts, graphs, and hard information, wanting to feel that they are making an informed, considered decision.

In the example on the following pages, we've highlighted the Impulsive Path, so you can see how it hops through the letter. The Analytical Path follows this same order, but every word is read along the way.

THE SILVER INVESTMENT OF THE DECADE

These 100 pesos silver dollars are priced to sell at only $8.75 each in quantity . . . way below normal rates. When you compare the price, choice, brilliant condition, and profit potential to any, and we do mean any, other silver coin investments, you will find this to be the best silver deal ever.

THE ULTIMATE IN PRIVACY

100 pesos silver dollars are private . . . completely exempt from the IRS reporting required of coin dealers on form 1099-B. Many investors demand complete privacy to buy and sell without a lot of government snooping . . . these coins are 100% fully exempt.

MAKE 1000% BY 1992?

Experts in many of the financial journals, people like Bill Kennedy of Western Monetary, the Aden Sisters, Howard Ruff, and others predict silver could blow the lid off and hit $25–$50 or even $100 per ounce by 1992 . . . if the financial fiasco boiling in Washington erupts. When this comes about, the 100 pesos could melt for as much as $70 per coin.

RICH IN SILVER CONTENT

These giant coins weigh nearly one ounce and are 72% pure in silver quality. The fact is, they offer 6 times as much silver for your money as BU Morgan silver dollars. And as silver prices climb in coming years, the value of these heavy coins should skyrocket. It's like having risk insurance on your silver investment. As incredible as it may seem, you can now own 6 of these big Mexican cartwheels in brilliant uncirculated condition for the price of just one common date U.S. Morgan dollar.

TIMING IS URGENT

The AMARK secret is beginning to leak out now . . . thus eliminating your chance of big profits. Don't wait until the cat's out of the bag! Buy now!! Next week or next month could be a red letter profit day for many astute silver investors who heed our advice today.

A CLASSIC FROM SILVER-RICH OLD MEXICO

As a big fan of the entire category of Mexican silver dollar size coins, I was excited when these factors came together . . . just at the right time . . . creating an unparalleled time to buy. Due to the latest Mexican financial crisis, you can buy coins at a small fraction above their actual intrinsic value—a remarkable paradox to say the least. And because this is the last of the great big high-silver content pesos coins in Mexican history . . . it's a classic!

Say It Again, Sam. And Again. And Again.

Can you fill in these blanks?

> *Pepsi-Cola hits (blank) (blank);*
> *(blank) (blank) (blank)—*
> *that's a lot!*

> *Lucky Strike means (blank) (blank).*

> *Double your (blank),*
> *double your (blank),*
> *with (blank), (blank), (blank) gum.*

> *At Burger King, you can (blank) (blank) (blank) (blank) (blank).*

> *It's (blank) time.*

These are very old advertising slogans that many people can still recall perfectly and instantly. Why? Did people make a special point of memorizing those slogans? Of course not! They learned and memorized this information automatically, as a result of massive repetition. In fact, that's one of only two ways that we accept new ideas and information as valid—through repetition. (The other way is shock.)

Let me give you an example: selling home security systems. A great many people invest in such systems immediately after their homes have been broken into. They accept the idea of the worth and importance of such a product thanks to the shock of having their home invaded, burglarized, maybe even vandalized. The only other way they will come to accept this idea and invest in a system is by being repetitively exposed to persuasive information.

In one of my businesses, I publish and distribute audiocassette courses that teach business, entrepreneurial, sales, negotiation, and self-improvement skills. These types of cassette publications have become immensely popular because they provide an effortless, convenient way to get repetitious exposure to new information so that acceptance and understanding occur. This same process that works so well in teaching is equally powerful in selling.

In public speaking, there is a time-honored axiom: tell 'em what you're going to tell 'em, tell 'em, tell 'em, then tell 'em what you've told 'em. I've expanded it to: tell 'em what you're going to tell 'em; tell 'em; tell 'em again, a little differently; tell 'em again, a little more differently; then tell 'em what you've told 'em. In fact, I try to tell 'em seven times. I do this in my speeches and seminars. I do it in my sales letters, too. I call it internal repetition.

In the same sales letter, you can convey your basic sales message and promise:

1. In a straightforward statement
2. In an example
3. In a story, sometimes called a "slice of life"
4. In testimonials
5. In a quote from a customer, expert, or other spokesperson
6. In a numbered summary

A "manufactured example" that uses all these methods appears on the following page.

4-ACES CARPET CLEANING SPECIALISTS
123 Success Street
Cleansville, USA 123456

Dear Briarwood Area Homeowner,

You've probably lived in your home for three, four, maybe even five years, and in that time a lot of "traffic" has taken its toll on your carpets.

We guarantee to make your carpeting look like new, or there's no charge for our services!

Here's how it works: we'll come to your home, by appointment. First, we'll test the "worst spot." If you judge that job successful, we'll do that whole room. You continue to be the judge, room by room. You pay only for what you approve. And, during the next 21 days, you get one room FREE for every three cleaned. For example, a typical Briarwood home with an # x # carpeted living room, a # x # carpeted family room and two # x # carpeted bedrooms will get one bedroom's carpeting CLEANED FREE!

Like new again—no matter what!

We were recently called to one home where, while the parents were away, the teenagers' "little party" had gotten out of control: beer stains, soda pop stains, ground-in mud and grime, and a few things we never definitely identified! Here's what that homeowner, Mrs. Trusting Parent on Elm Street, said after our visit:

"When I saw the living room carpet after the kids' party, I just knew we'd have to buy all new carpeting. I tried some carpet cleaner liquid I bought at the store, and it just made it worse. But, in just one hour, the guys from 4-Aces had it perfectly clean! I'm still amazed everytime I look at it!"

Act now—call us today at 239-ACES and . . .

1. Schedule a FREE Consultation and Cost Quotation
2. We'll clean your carpets room by room
3. You judge our job as we go
4. You pay only for the work you approve
5. You get one room FREE for every three charged
6. Your satisfaction is guaranteed

Hank, Bill, Tom, & Larry,
"The 4 Aces"

Move Your Reader Along with a Yes Sequence

Recently a hypnotherapist reminded me of a basic principle of persuasion: building a "yes momentum." You develop receptivity to your offer by giving your readers a sequence of knowns they can easily agree with and questions they can easily say "yes" to. This gets them in the habit of agreeing with you.

You might incorporate this idea in a sales letter by starting or ending each paragraph with a question, or using questions as subheads. Asking questions involves the reader.

Tease the Reader at the End of Each Page

First, a format tip: never end a page with a completed sentence. This gives your reader permission to stop reading right there. Instead, always end each page in the middle of a sentence, preferably right in the middle of an interesting or exciting phrase. This spurs the reader on to the next page where, once started, he or she is likely to finish.

In addition, you may want to add "teaser copy" at the bottom of each page. This is an opportunity to use a graphic device, by the way, such as simulated handwriting or yellow fake highlight. A blurb of teaser copy is something like this:

> The Author's 7 secrets for beating the stock market,
> revealed on the next page!

> How we saved $38,000 in repairs the first year—
> even though we were skeptics! See the next page!

Now, from these examples, did you pick up on the secret to creating good teaser copy? A teaser blurb is essentially another headline. In fact, it is a headline for the next page! So you use the principles for creating successful headlines to create your teaser blurbs, too.

REWRITE FOR STYLE

Beyond the mechanics, the teaser lines, and the readership paths lies the question of your letter's general strength of delivery. In this chapter we'll look at some of the most effective ways to make your letter stand out as "a good read."

INCREASE READERSHIP BY IMPROVING READABILITY

What is readability? The computer industry uses the term "user friendly." I think they apply this rather loosely, but it is supposed to mean that the computer is easy to use, uses everyday language, and does not require you to be a rocket scientist to operate it. I think sales letters should be reader friendly. That means the letter appears easy to read, is easy on the eye, uses everyday language, and doesn't require you to be a Harvard grad or a determined masochist to get through it.

A good copywriter creates this reader friendliness with a number of devices that nurse the reader along—that push, prod, pull, entice, and motivate. These devices include short, punchy sentences and even shorter nonsentences. You should also stick mostly to short paragraphs (ideally, those only three or four sentences long).

USE THE FIRST PARAGRAPH AS AN EXTENDED HEADLINE

Think of it this way: in the first paragraph, you sell the recipient on reading your letter; then in the letter, you sell your proposition. Here's an example of a poorly used first (and second) paragraph (in an otherwise reasonably good sales letter)—and a repaired version.

Emergency Memo for Preferred Clients

I would have taken the time to write you a personalized letter, but in this instance I believe that getting the information into your hands pronto is more important. Even our Marketing Department requested I bypass them and go directly to our most concerned silver investors.

You've probably been watching the silver market lately, and as you may have guessed, market indicators show that silver is getting ready to make a surge. But many of our silver buyers have been afraid to buy bullion due to possible IRS reporting, and have asked for our recommendation as the next best thing to buy for investors who value their privacy.

Here's my rewrite:

Emergency Memo for Preferred Clients Direct from Brent Lee, Research Department

*Market indicators show that silver is getting ready to make a surge! But many of our silver buyers have been afraid to buy bullion, due to possible IRS reporting, and have asked us for help. Now we have the answer: just what the doctor ordered for savvy silver investors who value their privacy—fully explained in this important letter!

BE ENTERTAINING

No, don't be *funny*. Outright humor rarely works in sales letters and is too difficult for anyone but an experienced pro to carry off. There are safer, surer paths to follow. On the other hand, you may not want to be funeral-serious throughout your letter, either. In fact, there's no such thing as too much interesting copy—the problem's not with the length. The problem is being boring.

Here's the beginning of a letter I sent to a group of people who travel incessantly (as I do). As you'll see, it is lighthearted; not comical, but not dead serious.

Last night, I left a Wake-Up-And-What-City-Am-I-In-And-What-Day-Is-This call at my hotel. Maybe I'm traveling just a little too much! How about you? Just recently, I've discovered a way to earn lots of money in our business without squeezing into the big silver tube and heading off

*Letter excerpt used courtesy of Chattanooga Coin Co., Box 80158, Chattanooga, Tennessee 37411.

for distant lands. If you'll give me 15 minutes of your time to read this letter thoroughly, I'll share every profitable detail with you right now!

A dead serious version of the same copy might look like this:

Tired of traveling? There is a way to earn lots of money in your business without travel. Read this letter and learn more about it.

Which is more fun to read?

APPEAL TO THE SENSES

Although we consciously think mostly in terms of sight, our more powerful subconscious system takes in input from all five senses all the time.

I believe that the reader's "whole mind" can best be stimulated by playing on as many of the five senses as possible.

Consider, for instance, the idea of selling a good, fast computer by describing the unpleasant experience of being the last person left working late, alone, in a big, dark, cold office. Remember, your sales-letter copy needs to make the reader visualize pictures and feel experiences.

USE BIG IMPACT WORDS AND PHRASES

Consider this incredible example of words on paper that absolutely command attention and evoke emotion:

There was a desert wind blowing that night. It was one of those hot dry Santa Anas that come down through the

mountain passes and curl your hair and make your
nerves jump and your skin itch. On nights like that every
booze party ends in a fight. Meek little wives feel the edge
of the carving knife and study their husbands' necks.
Anything can happen.

That's from the late, great mystery-novelist Raymond Chan-
dler. As a frustrated novelist myself, I love passages like that—and
I have found them useful in sales letters. And if you find writing
whole blocks of copy like that too tough, at least plug in "charged"
phrases here and there.

Here are a few such phrases I've found or thought up and
used in various sales letters:

- Serious as cancer
- Stronger 'n onions!
- Savage wind
- So overcome with frustration, he leans against the
  closed door of his office and silently screams

I've built up a fairly large card file of such phrases, culled from
advertising, television, novels, all sorts of sources. I suggest that you
do the same. These kinds of phrases add bursts of color to your copy.

MAKE YOUR LETTER REFLECT YOUR OWN PERSONAL STYLE

I admit here that I don't know how to tell you how to do this. I only
know that some letters have personality and others don't. Some
letters give you the feeling you're hearing from a real human
being, a unique individual; others don't.

The best sales-letter writers I know have their own unique styles. I can usually tell their work in my own incoming mail by this style, and I'm right about 90% of the time.

Let your own personality come into your letters. Sell in print as you would in person.

ANSWER QUESTIONS AND OBJECTIONS

Unanswered questions and unresolved concerns sabotage sales letters! By carefully countering every possible question and objection, you put the ultimate sales presentation on paper.

THE REASONS WHY NOT

In person-to-person selling, there is a step typically referred to as "overcoming objections." At some point, the prospect is going to raise one or (more likely) several objections, and it is up to the salesperson to counter or neutralize those objections effectively. Some salespeople welcome this exercise because they believe it indicates real interest on the prospect's part. Others fear and loathe this part of selling. But whatever the individual salesperson's past experience and attitude toward customer objections, they will come up in almost every sale, and they must be dealt with.

Live salespeople have several big advantages over the sales-letter writer in facing objections. First, they have the luxury of responding only to those objections raised by the individual customer. Second, they get immediate feedback to determine whether they have satisfied the customer with an answer or whether they need to tell more. Third, they can "box in" the customer to turn the objection-answering process into a sure sale. There is, for example, a selling tactic known as "draining the objections," in which salespeople list the objections on a pad before answering any. They keep asking "Anything else?" until the customer runs dry of objections. Then they ask, "If we can take care of all these concerns to your satisfaction—and I'm not sure that we can—but if we can, you will then want to go ahead with the XYZ tonight, right?" When the customer says "yes" to that, he or she is boxed in. There's no way I've found to duplicate that process in print.

Our sales letter does not have the luxury of responding only to the objections each recipient thinks of. The letter has to respond to every possible objection. Our letter does not get any feedback making it clear when "enough is enough," so it must do more than enough.

I've sat in meetings with clients and advertising pros and had them argue vehemently against raising any objections in a sales letter. Why put negative thoughts in a reader's mind? While I avoid overestimating a customer's intelligence, I try never to underestimate skepticism! Those marketers who think they can "hide" the objectionable issues are grossly underestimating the skepticism of customers. If they are going to think of anything, they are going to think of all the reasons not to buy.

As it happens, I've had great success with a copywriting formula that airs the likely objections for the customer, then answers them. The start of that copy block reads something like this:

> As attractive as this product/service/offer is, our marketing experts tell us that only about X% of the people receiving it will respond. Although that's okay with us from a business standpoint, it still bothers me personally. You see, I know how much the owners/users of our product/service/ offer benefit from it. I read their letters; I talk to them on the phone; I see them personally when they visit us; and hundreds/thousands/millions each year tell me that "(strong, brief customer quote)". Because of this, I just hate the thought of someone not getting our product/ service/offer because of some error or omission in our explanation. That's why I held a special brainstorming session with a group of our people just to try and figure out why you might say "no" to our free trial offer. After several hours, our group could think of only three possible reasons. Here they are:

After a setup like that, I would list each reason for not buying and then respond to it.

Another, more commonly used (and, I think, wimpier, though still effective) version of this formula is to include a page of "Frequently Asked Questions and Answers" with the sales letter. The anticipated objections are phrased as questions and answered.

In either case, the answers to most objections or questions should include most, and, in most instances, all of these items:

1. A direct answer.
2. A verifying testimonial comment, case history, or story.
3. A restatement of or reference to the guarantee/free trial offer.

13

SPARK IMMEDIATE ACTION

When you play the sales-letter game, you go up against some pretty difficult mathematics: X% of your letters never get delivered to the intended recipients, Y% of the letters are discarded unopened, Z% reach people who, for one reason or another, cannot or will not respond, no matter how good the offer is. But quite probably, the biggest group of nonrespondents are those who get the letter, look at the letter, read the letter, and intend to respond to the letter—but set it aside to do "later." All too often, "later" never happens.

THE MAÑANA ANTIDOTE:
HOW TO GET IMMEDIATE RESPONSE

In most cases, then, most of the response to a sales letter will come in almost immediately. Yes, there will be a "trickle effect," and you will get some response weeks or even months after mailing the letter—from people who set the letter aside, buried it under a pile of papers, waited until they could afford to respond, or had any of a number of other reasons to procrastinate. This trickle, though, is virtually insignificant in terms of the profitability of a letter campaign. You go to the bank with the immediate response. For this reason, you must give careful thought to every possible way you can increase the urge to respond immediately.

One of my mentors in copywriting used to tell me: "Imagine your letter being read by a guy in an apartment in Cleveland, in the midst of a ferocious winter storm, with gusting winds and snow outside at thigh height. You've got to get him so excited that he'll get out of the chair in front of the fireplace, bundle up, slog through the snow, go out to his cold car, and drive down to the post office to get a money order and a stamp to send his order in—rather than take the risk of waiting until tomorrow."

Of course, the job is rarely that tough, because customers can respond to most sales letters by phone, calling toll-free numbers and paying by credit card. Still, the idea is the same. Responding is sometimes inconvenient. Usually, your letter's recipient is busy and preoccupied with other matters. There is tremendous temptation to stop at a "conditional yes"—setting the letter aside with the intention of responding "tomorrow."

Your letter's job is to get the reader to respond right now.

Here are the seven most powerful ways I know of to stimulate immediate response:

1. Limited Availability

If you are honestly making an offer in which either the primary product or the premium or a discount or rebate is limited by availability, you can try to convince the recipient that "the race is on!"

2. Premiums

It is rare for the basic offer to be strong enough in and of itself to inspire immediate response from a satisfactory number of people. Because of this, I am a strong advocate of the use of premiums, and usually prefer a premium over a discount or rebate. It has often been my experience that the right premium offer can make as much as a 50% positive difference in response to a sales letter.

An example of both these strategies combined in a single letter comes from Bob Stupak, the creator of the Vegas World Hotel (now the Stratosphere) in Las Vegas—in my opinion, the shrewdest marketer that entire city has ever seen.

For years, Vegas World sold a package including lodging, drinks, entertainment, and a gambling bankroll for a set price through print ads, direct mail, and television. If you bought the package and went, as soon as you returned home you received an invitation to buy that same package again and use it in the future. Many people became repeat purchasers of these packages and came to realize that they could get one just about whenever they wanted it, so the usual urgency-building techniques—like an ordering deadline—no longer worked on those people. They became immune to those offers. As a result, Bob Stupak developed the letter that follows.

From the Desk of Bob Stupak

Dear Mr. and Mrs. Kennedy:

I am writing to just a fraction of my previous guests for this first-time offer. This is a test and may never be repeated again.

SIX DAY, FIVE NIGHT HAWAIIAN VACATION

I have entered into a contract with Holiday Travel of America, one of the nation's largest fully bonded wholesale travel agencies, and have paid in advance for over 1,000 Hawaiian vacation packages to present as gifts to my returning previous guests.

When you again accept your fabulous Vegas World invitation with us, we will immediately send you your documents for a wonderful Hawaiian vacation for two.

The next, lengthy paragraph describes the Hawaiian package. The letter then continues:

But please remember, this is a test and is being offered to only a fraction of our previous guests and may never be offered again. This offer is available only until Thursday, November 1st or until our allotted number of Hawaiian vacations is gone, whichever comes first, so I urge you to act quickly.

The next paragraphs describe the Vegas World package, making the important point that it is the same package at the same price as always.

There are several enclosures with this letter that reinforce the core offer and the premium. Does it work? Well, it got me! The morning it arrived in my mail at the office, I was busier than the proverbial one-armed paper hanger and certainly had no intention of buying another Vegas World package that day—but I stopped what I was doing, read the letter, got on the phone, and ordered immediately. Why?

1. I knew and trusted the company (Vegas World).
2. I liked the product (the Vegas World package).
3. I believed the urgency-building story (only 1,000 Hawaiian vacations available).
4. I found the premium exciting and desirable.

Duplicate those four factors in a sales letter, and you'll have a winner, too. In fact, I urge you to write those four factors down on a card or sheet of paper and keep it visible, wherever you work and will write your sales letters. If you engineer a selling environment where these four factors exist and can be carried over to your sales letter, you are virtually guaranteed success.

Here's a business-to-business sales letter example utilizing the same strategy, from a publisher of educational videotapes for use in sales training:

FREE TV AND VCR—BUT YOU MUST CALL NOW!

We've made a special purchase, direct from a major Japanese manufacturer, of just 250 19-inch color TV monitors with built-in VCRs. If purchased in a store, this model might cost you $499 to as much as $899. But you can get one free, as a gift, with your purchase of any one of our three new Video Training Systems described in the enclosed brochure. You already know the fantastic quality and effectiveness of our systems—you own at least one of them already. Now you can get one of our newest systems—plus a free TV/VCR. But you must act immediately. We have only 250 of these TV/VCRs and cannot obtain any more.

3. Deadlines

The deadline is the most basic and common urgency-builder. It can stand alone or be used in combination with any of the other strategies.

If your mailings are small, you'll give extra impact to the deadline date by having it handwritten or rubber-stamped on your letter. If quantity prohibits that, you might work with your artist and printer to simulate a handwritten or rubber-stamped appearance.

An insurance agent friend of mine was in the habit of mailing out 100 letters each week to cold prospects compiled from his local street directory, offering a free road atlas just for letting him quote prices on auto insurance. Typically, he'd get one, two, or three responses from each hundred—which, incidentally, is pretty darned good in such a situation. At my suggestion, he changed the letter to offer the free road atlas only if the recipient responded by a certain date; the date was rubber-stamped in red the letter. His response went from between 1% and 3% to 8%.

4. Multiple Premiums

I've often found that if one is good, two is better! When a premium offer proves successful, it's usually smart to then test a double-premium offer.

A company selling cleaning, deodorizing, and safety chemicals via sales letters experienced considerable success when it added the offer of a free locking storage cabinet with a certain-size order received within 15 days. When I saw the dramatic increase in response that the addition of this premium caused, I suggested testing a double premium. The company then offered one cabinet with an $X order or two cabinets with a larger $Y order. While the overall response percentage remained virtually the same, the average order size increased by nearly 30%!

5. Discounts for Fast Response, Penalties for Slow Response

This strategy is used a lot in the seminar business. Take a look at the next few seminar brochures that cross your desk and you'll undoubtedly see pricing schedules that look like this:

ENROLL BY JANUARY 15: $149 per person

ENROLL AFTER JANUARY 15 BUT BEFORE FEBRUARY 20: $199 per person

AT-THE-DOOR (if available): $229 per person

This same strategy could be applied to advance-order offers tied to new, soon-to-be-released products; any kind of event tickets or passes; subscriptions or subscription renewals; and other offers.

6. Sweepstakes and Contests

Who hasn't received an envelope with Ed McMahon's smiling face on the outside? ("You may be our next millionaire winner!") Sweepstakes and contests have entry deadlines, so they spark immediate response. They are used not only by subscription agencies like American Family and Publishers Clearing House, but also by car companies, industrial manufacturers, service businesses, and others. They are admittedly expensive but seem to repay their investments many times over in increased response.

7. Ease of Responding

Essentially, the easier it is for the person to respond, the better. Offering a toll-free number always boosts response tremendously, and depending on the nature of your business, letter recipients, and economics, having that number manned 24 hours a day, seven days a week and/or enclosing preaddressed response cards or envelopes may prove beneficial.

Surprisingly, including postage-paid response devices rarely enhances response enough to justify the added expense. If you are going to do this, you should test it both ways—you may discover that the cost is unwarranted.

You should also consider inviting response by fax, with a form included for that purpose; via your Web site, entering information there and/or downloading information; even via e-mail.

THE CREATIVE P.S.

Every sales letter needs a P.S.—do not consider your efforts complete until you have composed one. The P.S. can make or break your letter!

USE THE P.S. TO STIMULATE READERSHIP

Yes, many people skip to the end of the letter first. Some want to look at the signature, to try to identify who is writing to them. Others are just perverse—they also read the end of a mystery novel before buying it, and they eat their dessert first. Their perversity is your opportunity! By properly summarizing the offer/promise in your P.S., you can inspire the recipient to dig in and read the entire letter, or simply add an extra incentive to respond.

P.S.: Even if your reader has read the text in the "proper" sequence, the P.S. serves as a high-impact "second headline" you can ill afford to ignore!

Step

15

CHECK THE CHECKLISTS

You have now written several drafts, and you've made heaven only knows how many changes and corrections in the surviving draft. If you wind up working the way I do, your draft will look like the homework you used to claim your dog ate.

I travel quite a bit, some years well over 150,000 air miles, and I for one am glad that pilots operate with checklists. After all, how many times have you simply forgotten to do something you know you should do? (Yesterday, I got out of my car without putting it into "Park" or turning off the engine; the car lurched against the parking block and sat there groaning, grumbling under its breath about its idiot owner. Obviously, I'm a big believer in checklists.) This step is the way to be certain you incorporate as many successful strategies, formulas, and techniques as possible in your sales letter. It is sort of a midcourse correction. You are about halfway through the entire system, the process of writing your sales letter, and this is a good time to make a number of little adjustments.

16

USE GRAPHIC ENHANCEMENT

Now it's time to do a draft of your letter on your PC and start to jazz it up with graphic devices.

GIVE YOUR LETTER AN EASY-TO-READ APPEARANCE

The sales-letter writer should collaborate closely with the type-setter or typist, layout artist, and printer to use as many "graphic devices" as possible to make the long copy look (perhaps decep-tively) easy to read.

The truth of the matter is that today's consumer is lazier than ever. Consider the TV remote control, the microwave, the cellular telephone, passive exercise machines. Look around: we don't do things, we have things done for us. We don't want it fast—we want it now!

To make a long sales letter look like an easier and faster read, these are the graphic devices I like best:

1. Bullets • • • • • •
2. Numbering: 1, 2, 3, etc.
3. <u>Underlining</u>
4. **Boldfacing**
5. *Varied* type
6. Simulated handwriting—in the margins, in the P.S.
7. Boxes
8. Lines made of asterisks ******************
9. Yellow overprint (Your printer can use yellow ink to simulate sloppy markings made with a yellow highlighter pen.)
10. Screens (i.e., washes of a light dot pattern over the text). Over a paragraph or two, you can use a gray screen if printing in black, or a pastel screen from your primary accent color (pink from red, for instance).
11. Photographs with type running around them
12. Subheads . . . lots and lots of subheads!

Contrary to what many people in the advertising business believe, these choices about graphic devices should not be left up to the typesetters and artists. The person who writes the copy must have direct involvement in suggesting, considering, and deciding on the use of these devices.

The main purpose of these devices is not to improve the aesthetic appearance of the letter; it is to add "voice inflection" to the copy—and the copywriter is best qualified to choose what to emphasize and how to emphasize it.

You'll find value in building up an "idea file" from the sales letter and mail you receive, so you can show other project partici- pants exactly what you want.

Step

17

REWRITE FOR PASSION! EDIT FOR CLARITY!

Here is yet another chance to rewrite your piece; this time the accent is on the unpredictable, passionate side of your offer.

HOW TO PUT PASSION INTO YOUR SALES LETTER

Sales-letter writing is no place for pure, cold, hard logic, even if you are selling a logical proposition to presumably logical people. I don't care what business you're in or who your prospects or customers are, they buy by emotion and then justify their choice with logic. My speaking colleague, the famous sales trainer and motivational speaker Zig Ziglar calls that "emotional logic."

Even in very technical fields, you do not find too many hard-core analytical personalities in sales positions. These "cold fish" just can't make it in selling. Most successful sales-people, again—even in highly technical fields—have amiable, friendly, enthusiastic personalities. They are "people people." This gives us valuable clues about the necessary personality of a sales letter.

"Cold fish" sales letters rarely work. The purely factual approach fails almost every time it's used. A sales letter needs an enthusiastic personality—and because it is ink on paper, not warm flesh and blood, the letter has to work harder at being enthusiastic. That means that what will seem overly expressive when you write it will still wind up understated when it's read.

Consider this: most columnists, pundits, and political analysts would agree, in principle, that electing an individual to serve as president of the United States should be a serious-as-cancer business. Yet in the 1988 campaign, what was every analyst bemoaning after the conventions produced their nominees? The lack of a passionate advocate. Reporters, insiders, and other "experts" had to watch as two less-than-compelling media figures slugged it out . . . and sales of No-Doz tablets among political commentators hit new highs.

No matter what people may think about their own attention spans or those of their prospects, the number-one sin in marketing in general (and sales-letter writing in particular) is being boring. The desirable opposite, I think, is being exciting, passionate—even a little wild! Are you eager to pull the passion from within yourself—to channel it into your sales letter? Here's an exercise I suggest you try. Assume you're writing a letter to someone with whom you're having an illicit affair. In the letter, you're going to convince your lover—who is slightly more conservative than you are, but who has shown signs of having a wild side—to take an entire week off to be with you. You must convince the person to make some excuse to be away from work and responsibilities for that week, to take all the risks inherent in this action in order to sneak away to the Bahamas with you— where you will have free use of a friend's villa, right on the beach. Use as many pages as you like. (You've got a sales job and a half here!)

You can be bold, daring, even shocking. You can be poetic; you can be romantic; you can be colorful in your descriptions of the sun, the sea, the land, the stars, the breeze, the ocean smell. Where will you go? What will you do when you get there? Anticipate the objections and eliminate them as you go. Make huge promises! Create an overwhelming desire in your reader to go with you on that trip—no matter what the risk!

I conducted this exercise in a direct-marketing seminar once; everyone in the group was participating eagerly except for one man. He came up to me after the seminar and told me he'd had problems with the whole idea.

"First of all," he said, "I've been married to the same woman for thirty-eight years. In all that time, I haven't even thought about an affair. And there's certainly nothing exciting about my relationship. Second, I own a specialty electronic-parts business. We sell parts to manufacturers of electronic products. Our business is boring and so is theirs. We talk to each other in part numbers. No romance there. I don't think this is for me."

As I quizzed him about his business, I found that his was one of about a dozen similar companies in this funny little industry, all pursuing the same clientele—in, incidentally, the same dull, dreary, traditional way. The only two things his customers supposedly cared about were price and reliable, on-time delivery.

I'm a little embarrassed to admit it, but I took this fellow out after the seminar to a rather raucous bar I know and popped a few drinks into him. I wanted to loosen him up, try to get his motor revving. I challenged him to come up with a passionate, lively sales letter to send to companies he didn't have as customers, and to send just 10 or 20 at a time.

He came back a couple of months later, the proud and happy creator of a marketing revolution in his once-dreary little industry. His sales letter was printed in red ink, on hot pink paper, with the headline:

**69 Things You Can Do after Work
When You Are Absolutely Free of Worry
about Whether or Not Your Part
Will Arrive on Time Tomorrow.**

In the first paragraph, he quickly told the reader about his huge inventory, 24-hour-a-day ordering service, air-courier shipments, and guarantee of on-time delivery. The rest of the three-page letter was, sure enough, devoted to a list of 69 things a worry-free manager might do with an evening. Some were funny; some were ordinary, but pleasant; some were outrageous; a few were a little "blue." Enclosed with the letter was a copy of his regular parts catalog with a huge hot pink sticker affixed to the front: "BORING BUT NECESSARY."

"Well," he said proudly, "what do you think?"

What do you think? Frankly, I was afraid he was going to tell me a horror story about how he had mailed these things and been laughed out of town. But the truth was, he'd sent out 100 of these pink-and-red motivators, gotten 22 telephone calls from amused (and amazed) recipients, and received 18 separate first-time orders, all of which converted to long-term accounts. The campaign was worth over $200,000 in new business to him that year.

Although his situation was unique, the episode introduces a valuable lesson about putting passion into a sales letter: no matter what your business may be, you can find something to get excited about. If you can't romanticize your product or service or its direct benefits, you've got to be able to create excitement out of the feelings of owning it or using it, or the enjoyment of the money or time it saves. Find something for the reader to get excited about! It doesn't matter what your topic is: there is a way to give your sales story a passion injection.

Consider the example on the following page.

WHEN ARE YOU GOING TO GET TIRED ENOUGH OF BEING IN DEBT TO DO SOMETHING ABOUT IT?

Dear Friend,

You're getting this letter because—incredibly—it's a matter of <u>public record</u> that you're in financial difficulty!!! I say "dear friend," because six years ago, I was where you are now . . . embarrassed. Frustrated. Hounded by creditors. Paranoid. Defensive. Angry. Wondering whether I'd ever get ahead. Hating the ring of the phone.

That experience motivated me to become a <u>researcher</u>. In one year, six years ago, I spent over 300 hours at the public library, at the law library, interviewing accountants and CPAs and tax experts and attorneys. From all that, I developed a nine-point step-by-step strategy for getting out of debt once and for all. It worked for me. It can work for you. Here are some of the nine steps:

1—STOP creditors' collection actions (in 90% of the cases, without bankruptcy, without an attorney!)

3—PROTECT your personal and family property from creditors

5—"DAMAGE CONTROL" for your credit rating and credit reports, so you can rebuild fast

7—Establish a spare time, weekend, 2nd income of $300 to $500 per month, from your choice of a dozen different proven plans

All nine of my steps can save your financial life!

My information <u>will</u> stop the wolves from barking at your door . . . protect your possessions . . . give you time to breathe and think . . . reorganize your payments to an amount you really can handle . . . put more money in your pocket . . . give you knowledge, control, confidence and peace of mind. How about a good night's sleep—for a change? Here I am, my friend . . . at the end of the tunnel . . . shining a beacon of light back toward you, saying "C'mon, let me help you escape your Debt Trap!"

Right now, you can hear all about my nine step system just by making a simple telephone call to 1-900-000-0000. I've recorded a message especially for you! You'll hear my personal debt-to-riches story . . . how my strategy works . . . and how you can get and try it yourself on a satisfaction guaranteed basis. There is a charge for the call: $2.00 for the first minute and $1.00 for each additional minute which will appear on your phone bill—but this is a very small cost to invest in getting debt free!

AGGRESSIVE EDITING

Now that we've added a splash of color and passion, it's time to get a little ruthless with your text.

Aggressive editing means cutting out every word or phrase that fails to advance, strengthen, or reinforce your basic sales story. You're not editing to shorten. You are editing to clarify, and that will automatically shorten the letter.

For example, a sales-letter draft had this wording:

> We have many imitators, but no one who matches the quality of our products, our eight years of leadership in this industry, or our guarantee . . . .

In the aggressive editing process, this was changed to:

> Our many imitators can't match . . . .

See how much faster that gets to the point? How much clearer it makes the letter?

This process may take days. You may need to attack your text, set the draft aside, then come back to it hours later and edit some more. But do it!

Step

18

COMPARE YOUR DRAFT TO EXAMPLES

I like to put my draft side by side with good examples, to compare and check for ways to improve my letter. This book is full of examples useful for this purpose.

Don't just use one letter for comparison—find several that allow you to isolate your word's strengths and weaknesses.

Does your letter's text flow as smoothly as the letters referenced? Is it as compelling? Does it speak to its target audience as well? Is it structurally as sound? Is it as easy to understand? Does it excite a potential reader to action as effectively?

When you've spent a good chunk of time reviewing how your letter stands up to the others reproduced in this book, consider incorporating changes and revisions based on your observations.

COMPARE YOUR DRAFT TO EXAMPLES

19

PRETEST

The draft developed in the privacy of your PC is ready for comments from the outside world. Turn on your office copier, pass the text around, and get ready for feedback!

NO-COST PRETESTING

These days even a relatively small direct-mail test of, say, 5,000 to 10,000 units can cost a small fortune. That's why I like to pretest (at a cost of zero dollars, of course). I find glitches that can still be repaired before mailing, and get a better feel for the probable success or failure of the letter. In a few cases, the pretest feedback has been so bad that I've trashed the entire letter and started over. In most cases, nothing that drastic happens, but a few final opportunities for improvement are detected.

The following are the best no-cost ways to pretest a sales letter.

1. Read the Letter Aloud

It should "flow" smoothly, conversationally, whether read silently or aloud. If you find tongue twisters or hang-ups, fix them. The sales letter must read easily.

2. Read the Letter to Several People Who Might Be Typical Customers for the Offer

I know one highly paid copywriter of sales letters geared to blue-collar men. He routinely takes his letters down to a neighborhood bar, buys a round of beers for everybody, and then reads them his sales-letter drafts. He welcomes their comments and ideas. But he's most interested in the secret acid test they have no idea they're participating in. If some of them start asking how they can get the product or service described in the letter, he knows the basic approach is sound. If the letter is exciting enough to move people from the critic's corner to the cash-register line, he knows he's got a winner.

Sometimes this type of input can lead to dramatic results. I gave one client's direct-mail package—a short letter, a full-color catalog, and a response device—to a few typical customers; they looked through it all, but then they had a zillion questions! So the good news was: it got some motors running. The bad news was: it left lots of unanswered questions that could prevent response. As a result, I created a new eight-page sales letter that answered all of their questions. Response is up almost 15% since the use of the new letter began.

3. Have A Young Child Read the Letter Aloud to You

Any words or phrases the youngster has difficulty with should probably be changed. I've used this strategy for many years; however, it is now more important than ever.

I know that many will instantly object to this idea. Perhaps you think your customers are "smarter than the average bear." If so, consider an article from *DM News* (September 15, 1989) headlined: "Look Who's Opening Your Direct Mail—And Can They Read It?" It reads, in part, as follows: "Over 27 million adults cannot read. An additional 46 million are either functionally illiterate or marginally illiterate. This means that one out of every three adult Americans lacks a skill level required to be satisfactorily literate in today's society."

Of course, the important question is: are your customers literate? The article goes on: "Many marketing professionals feel that this incidence of illiteracy does not pertain to their own potential customers, particularly when mailing business-to-business. A word of caution: illiteracy is not restricted to those standing in the unemployment lines. . . . Sadly, perhaps, corporate America, in order to fill available job openings, has found it necessary to lower its employment requirements. Others who are illiterate have found ways to bypass the system and secure employment without detection."

It's my most current, admittedly curmudgeonly observation that the younger-than-30 crowd is even less literate, less intelligent, and cursed with poorer attention spans than the rest of us. If you are writing to MTVers, you are writing to nonreaders.

I believe that mysterious failures of creatively and technically sound sales letters may very well be due, at least in part, to this large, growing, and somewhat hidden functional illiteracy. This is a strong mandate for lowest-common-denominator copywriting.

Beyond the straightforward illiteracy issue is what I call the Sophistication Trap: stubbornly believing that your customers are more sophisticated than they really are.

Some of the most talented, highly skilled, and best-paid copywriters on the planet create the full-page, copy-i direct-response ads that appear in the *National Enquirer* and similar tabloids. Some of these copywriters earn fees and royalties of $25,000 to $100,000 per ad. To command that kind of money, you just have to be good. And for an advertiser to pay that kind of money, there have to be outstanding results. So if you want to go to a school of profitable copywriting tutored by the best and the brightest, pick up a copy of the *National Enquirer*. Skip the articles about the invading Martians impregnating talk show hosts— but study the ads!

If you choose to stick with the bias that your customers are much smarter and more sophisticated than that, I believe that choice will cost you a great deal of money.

First of all, there are a lot of closet *National Enquirer* readers out there—just take a look at the circulation figures! Second, no matter who your customers are, they are part of the buying public reached and swayed by TV commercials, which are now geared to a sixth-grade reading level. Butcher, baker, candlestick maker, doctor, lawyer, CEO—they're all people who respond to the same basic motives and appeals. And the key word there is "basic." Regardless of who you are addressing your copy to, it is better to err on the side of simplicity. (Bear in mind P. T. Barnum's famous remark about how no one ever went broke overestimating the ignorance of the American public. Lots of people have gone broke overestimating the sophistication of their customers.)

Step

20

BRING YOUR LETTER
TO LIFE

Finally—you're free to have your edited draft prepared exactly as you intend to send it out, on the typewriter, PC, or typesetting equipment. In other words, you can now pretend you are getting it ready for the printer. Think of this as your "dry run" or "dress rehearsal."

This is an exciting step because your letter comes to life before your eyes! What do you think of the current state of your project?

21

CHANGE GRAPHIC ENHANCEMENTS

Meet with your typesetter, layout artist, and printer to discuss the graphic devices you've plugged in and solicit their ideas.

This is also the time to work on the design of any enclosures going with the letter: coupons, certificates, product photos, or reply cards. Whatever you select, be absolutely certain that you like it, and that it appeals to your target readers. Changes after this stage are expensive and frustrating. Think twice.

22

EDIT AGAIN

Oops! Did you mean to write that? Wasn't the page break supposed to come farther down the sheet? Why did you choose to print the text in that hard-to-read color? What did you have in mind when you chose that typeface? Why is the headline hardly distinguishable from the rest of the letter?

This is a painful step. Nobody likes it. But you will notice things to change in this supposedly finished form, things that you missed previously. Bite the bullet and make the changes. You don't want anything less than a completely compelling sales letter.

(Once you've accepted the idea of making these changes, it's probably as good a time as any to repeat Step 15, Check the Checklists.)

23

MAIL A MOCK-UP

Things seem to be all set. It's off to the printer, right?

Wrong.

Now is the time for you to put together the best mock-up of the entire mailing that you can, with all the enclosures, then mail it to yourself. Your objective here is to receive it, see it, and handle it in the context of your normal stack of mail.

This may seem like a needlessly time-consuming chore, but it is perhaps the most important of the later steps. If your piece is of such a size that it will be roughed up and damaged by the post office, you should know that. If your piece does not compare well to the other mail you receive on an average day, you should know that. If your piece is meant to convey a "personalized" feeling, and it winds up looking like the rest of the "junk mail," you should know that.

You have worked too hard and spent too much time developing your letter to send it out without determining exactly how it will appear in its actual selling environment. Take the time to produce a mock-up and mail it. Your prospective customers will likely look much less charitably on the receipt of your letter than you do, but you will at least have something approaching a "real-life" test of your letter's initial appearance and effectiveness.

24

THE COOL OFF

You probably don't want to hear this, but the best thing for you to do once you receive your mock-up is—nothing. At least for a few days. The reason? You need to win back some objectivity. That quality is probably in pretty short supply now.

The more you work with your sales letter, the more likely you are to fall in love with it—see its beauties but not its blemishes. Also, you're going to get impatient with this admittedly lengthy—but effective—system. For these reasons, a three- to five-day cooling-off period is a good idea.

I confess that I sometimes work under such intense deadline pressure that I skip this step, even several of these last steps; I think my finished work in those situations suffers a little as a result. However, I would welcome the luxury of extra time to restore my objective judgment. If you have the time, take the time.

25

GET SECOND OPINIONS

I believe in getting second opinions, within certain very definite limits. You may have gotten such opinions earlier in this process, as part of pretesting. It won't hurt to get them again, now that you have done a great deal more work. The more experienced your contact, the better the advice you receive is likely to be.

GETTING AN EXPERT SECOND OPINION

What's an expert? Tough question. Everybody recognizes how unqualified everybody else is to opine on a matter, but no one considers himself unqualified to do so. (Consider that several surveys have shown something close to 70% of all licensed drivers to consider themselves "above average"—a statistical impossibility!) There is certainly no shortage of available opinions. Unfortunately, most are at best worthless and at worst dangerous.

Many people in direct marketing develop their own little networks of peers and colleagues they can bounce ideas, copy, and drafts off of in search of valid feedback. If you write a lot of sales letters, you need to develop such a network. If you don't know appropriate people, I'd suggest setting about meeting them. Seek out your local Direct Marketing Club and attend its meetings. Seek out your peers in national, state, and local trade associations who are aggressive, progressive marketers. And get a copy of the classic self-improvement book *Think and Grow Rich* by Dr. Napoleon Hill; study his ideas about forming a "mastermind group." There you'll find a little blueprint for your own creative alliance.

In the meantime, this book has been designed to serve as a consultant to you and to offer input on your sales letters.

Finally, I'd like to offer you a little personal assistance. On the next page, you'll find one of my Critique Certificates, which entitles you to submit one printed piece—such as a sales letter—for your business, for my personal review and comment. We routinely charge no less than $100 to $200 per critique, so this is a very real $100 to $200 value. It's probably the only time in your life you'll ever buy an inexpensive book and find $100 stuck inside it!

And it's very possible that redeeming it will prove even more valuable to you.

26

GIVE IT THE
FINAL REVIEW

This is it—the last chance to tinker and tighten. Take the time to find a quiet, peaceful place and scrutinize your letter just one more time.

GIVE IT THE FINAL REVIEW

Step

27

GO TO PRESS

Give it to the printers—but don't give up control. Make sure your concept stays intact. If you're dealing with a complex mailing or large quantity, check proofs and blue lines personally and carefully. Changes during this period—from the time you hand over the mechanicals to the time you give the OK for the work to go on press—fall into two categories: printer errors (PEs) and author alterations (AAs).

After following the exhaustive review and double-check procedures outlined in this book, there's very little likelihood you're going to decide to rewrite paragraphs now. But if you do, be prepared to pay—a lot. AAs are expensive, and you should only indulge in them if you find a glaring and damaging mistake. At this point, moving commas from inside the quotation marks to outside isn't the best use of your resources.

PEs, however, are another story. If you wanted yellow underlining and got a dull orange, make some noise and don't let the printer talk you into letting it go "as is." If the photos have uneven color values, tell the printer to go back and do the job again. If you selected a certain paper stock/color/size and are told it will be "easier for everybody" if you use what "everyone else uses," raise a stink about it. You're paying the bill. You're calling the shots. If the letter doesn't deliver, you will be the one to get hurt. Have it your way.

Of course, correcting PEs—errors arising from printer mistakes—should not cost you anything extra. Nevertheless, it is not uncommon for a few such items to sneak onto your bill once the job is complete. Printers do this to see if you are really paying attention. Don't let them down; show them that you are.

Step

28

MAIL!

At last—it's time to get your letters out the door. But before you do, take the time to ask yourself a few key questions. Most of the topics addressed here have probably been ironed out in earlier steps— but if, once you review them, you find yourself reassessing, for instance, your list selection or your mailing method, you may want to make a change now.

TIPS FOR MAILING TO SPECIAL GROUPS

Who are you mailing to? And how? No one mailing approach is right for all audiences.

NARROW-MARKET MAILINGS

Some companies do many small-quantity mailings aimed at narrowly selected segments of their own customer or prospect lists. An office supply firm, for instance, might isolate only its customers who own PCs for a special offer on related supplies, an equipment upgrade, or a trade-in program. When conducting such highly specialized mailings (usually to fewer than a thousand recipients), you may find the ideas listed here helpful. Used properly, they can increase response tremendously.

Use Real Stamps

Not metered postage. Some pros even use commemorative stamps when possible. Stamps convey a personal feel; a metered imprint says, "mass mailing."

Type the Envelopes

Or address them by hand. Or have ink-jet or computer imprinting done that perfectly mimics typewriting. Do not use labels unless absolutely unavoidable—and, if you do, then forget all about "sneaking up on 'em," and load up your envelope with bold teaser copy designed to compel the recipient to open it.

Use Rubber Stamps

A rubber-stamped imprint like FIRST CLASS MAIL or URGENT! or REQUESTED INFORMATION ENCLOSED will deliver impact. This idea, like the first two, contributes a person-to-person look to the envelope that increases its likelihood of surviving the junk mail sort—and whatever survives that "first cut" is a much better candidate to be opened and receive prompt attention.

Consider Non-Postal Delivery

UPS, Federal Express, messenger services, Western Union—all these delivery media have been used successfully with sales letters.

While these methods are expensive, they are fast, reliable, and virtually guarantee that your letter gets to the right person, opened, and read.

Consider Innovative Packaging

You might opt for extra bulky envelopes, bubble-bags, boxes, tubes, or other "odd" packages or enclosed objects as a way of commanding attention. One campaign used cassette players inside stuffed toy bears, with an audiocassette sales message waiting for the recipient. The bears were delivered by courier to the prospects. Two hundred such deliveries were made; 140 responses came in; and the marketer eventually did business with over 50 of the 200 prospects!

SUCCESS TIPS FOR BIG MAILINGS

There are many times when companies mail thousands, tens of thousands, even hundreds of thousands of units of a given mailing. With these quantities, the personalization techniques outlined here simply cannot be used.

Frankly, there are very few effective ways to enhance the effectiveness of such mailings—beyond, of course, writing the very best copy possible. However, there are a few tips you can follow.

Avoid Self-Defeating Address Designations

OCCUPANT. SALES MANAGER. POSTAL PATRON. When you see these or similar titles on your mail, what is your first reaction? If you're like most of us, the answer is simple: throw it away. This kind of addressing screams "junk mail!" The extra costs involved in actual name addressing usually represent a very good investment. If this is not practical for you, then try some imaginative addressing.

> To the BUSY FAMILY that lives at
> 123 Cherry Hill Lane
> Anytown, Ohio 00000

> To the CONCERNED PARENTS living at 456 Main Street
> Smallville, Vermont 00000

> To the PERSON WHO MUST INCREASE SALES for XYZ
>   Enterprises, Inc.
> 123 Business Street
> Metropolis, Texas 00000

Use Strong Teaser Copy on the Envelope Exterior

If you cannot simulate the look of a personal letter with stamps, individual addressing, and so forth, you might as well go to the other extreme: openly and clearly "confessing" that you are writing with some kind of offer, and saying something that commands the attention and interest of the recipient.

Consider Using Celebrity Identification

Of course, this is not right for all mailings, but there is a reason American Family uses Ed McMahon so prominently in its campaigns: to draw instant attention, as well as a measure of recognition and credibility, to the mailing piece. You too can hire an appropriate national or local celebrity, use the person's name and photo on your envelopes.

DIFFERENT WEAPONS

Different targets require different weapons. Take the time to analyze your target carefully—to understand your customer. Then pick the best possible weapons and act decisively.

CONGRATULATIONS!

These are the exact same 28 steps that I walk through every time I craft a new sales letter, and they are the same steps that I teach in my lectures and seminars on direct marketing. I sometimes call it a "miracle system" because I have seen many people with no formal training, background, or experience in advertising—and with minimal writing talent—sit down, follow these steps, and put together letters that get fantastic results. I know this system can work miracles for you, too!

SECTION III

The Most Versatile Sales Tool of All

Now that you've learned the Ultimate Sales Letter system and have it at your disposal, you'll want to get the maximum value from it. There are eight major ways we can use these kinds of sales letters for our own businesses and for clients; we'll look at each in this chapter.

1. To Create Qualified Leads

In-person cold calling has become prohibitively expensive and leads to high salesforce turnover. Cold-call telemarketing is also expensive and discouraging to telemarketers. Salespeople need qualified leads—it's that simple!

Once a good sales letter is developed and proved effective in generating qualified leads for your salespeople, you have the most controllable, manageable, and predictable lead generator in existence. There are, of course, many other ways to generate leads. Trade shows or mall exhibits work, but produce huge surges of leads in a few days, not a consistent flow. Media advertising of one kind or another can be used to provide leads, but results will vary tremendously based on all sorts of uncontrollable factors: day of the week, position on a page, the TV program running opposite your commercial, and so on.

A letter campaign that reliably produces, say, three leads per hundred units mailed will just about always produce at that level. The inherent variables of other media do not interfere with a letter campaign.

When someone picks up the phone and calls you in response to your sales letter, you know you've got a pretty qualified prospect!

2. To Support Telemarketing

Many businesses with active outbound telemarketing operations find that sending a sales letter, then following up with the telephone call, works much better than a cold telephone call by itself. The letter paves the way. It gives the telemarketer a reason for calling. It provides the interested prospect with reference information to refer to during the conversation.

This works whether the purpose of the phone call is to make an appointment or to make a sale.

A good example of this kind of letter appears on the facing page.

3. To Create Store Traffic

There's a Cadillac dealer in our area who mails a sales letter to me at least once a month, announcing some type of sale or event going on at the dealership. (I assume I'm on the list by virtue of owning a Lincoln Continental and/or living in a certain zip code.) These letters are designed to create traffic to the dealership. They are obviously working or I wouldn't keep getting them. Just about any retail business could certainly copy and use such an approach.

I know of one occasion where this kind of sales-letter campaign actually built a business from scratch. A deli and restaurant targeted all of the offices and businesses nearby, including many offices in high-rise towers, and used a sales letter to reach them. I don't have access to that letter anymore, but it went something like this:

WHO SAYS THERE'S NO SUCH THING AS A FREE LUNCH?

To introduce you to our huge, delicious sandwiches made to order with fresh deli meats and imported cheeses, we're

**"A money-saving message
exclusively for
small company CEOs . . ."**

Dear Beleaguered Business Owner,

I say "beleaguered" because I know you are surrounded by taxes—payroll taxes, income taxes, sales taxes, taxes, taxes and more taxes!!! Well, I have some incredibly good news for you:

In the last 6 months, right here in (name-of-city), our company has helped 164 businesses reduce their property taxes. We've helped over 100 even get rebates! We believe we can do the same for you.

Best of all, there is no charge for our service—unless and until we put money in your bank account!

It will take me less than 30 minutes to . . .

1. Explain this service and our other business services to you

2. Look at just four statistics in your financial statements, to determine the probability of us saving you money

One of my associates will be calling you in the next few days to arrange an appointment that is convenient for you. Please ask your receptionist or secretary to put through the call from DOLLAR-SAVERS INC., so we can get together soon.

Thank you,

John Q. Dollar

John Q. Dollar
President
Dollar-Savers, Inc.

P.S. Remember—the sooner we get to talk to you, the sooner we can work to reduce your tax burden!

going to give you a free lunch—no strings attached—no other purchase necessary. Come by yourself, bring the whole gang—from now until April 1, everybody gets a free sandwich!

The letter then continued with several short paragraphs describing the deli's specialty sandwiches, location, hours, and credit cards honored.

Of course, people bought drinks, side salads, and desserts, and the profit on those items helped offset the true cost of the free sandwiches. And the owner calculated that "buying his clientele" for a couple of months this way would be faster and cheaper than a longer-term commitment to all sorts of media advertising. He was right. By the time he had mailed only 300 letters, he had given away nearly twice that many sandwiches—and satisfied enough people that his repeat business every day jammed that little restaurant to its seams.

4. To Stimulate Referrals

This is an underused category of sales letter that I find particularly fascinating. I teach marketing techniques to dentists and chiropractors throughout the United States and Canada and have devised many referral-stimulation letters for their use. Most of my clients get very good results from using them. (See the letters that follow.)

Mr. Dan Kennedy
Empire Communications
5515 N. 7th Street
Phoenix, AZ 85014

Dear Mr. Kennedy:

We've come up with a great way to treat your friends as well as yourself.

Just give the coupons below to two friends or business associates who haven't yet tried Courtyard. Each coupon entitles them to a free weekend night at any Courtyard Hotel just for spending one night with us. Now that's a sure way to win friends overnight.

And there's more. Once a coupon is used by a new Courtyard guest, we'll send you a voucher in return that's good for a half-price night. So if both coupons are used, you also get a free night.

It's our way of thanking you for introducing your fellow business travelers to all the features Courtyard has to offer. From the spacious rooms and king-size beds to the whirlpool and friendly staff. You know from experience that Courtyard is always ready to make everyone's stay a pleasure.

And with this offer, we're also ready to make it free. The attached coupons, which can only be used by someone other than yourself, are good through December 30, 1989. And the vouchers you receive in return are valid through April 1, 1990.

So tear off the coupons now and give them away.

Of course, you've now come to the only problem with this offer: who are you going to give them to? Have fun deciding!

Sincerely,

Brent Andrus

Brent Andrus
V.P., Marketing and Sales

Detach coupons here and give them to two friends.

To redeem, stay one night and present this coupon at check-in for your free weekend night voucher. Call for exact locations and reservations 1-800-321-2211.	To redeem, stay one night and present this coupon at check-in for your free weekend night voucher. Call for exact locations and reservations 1-800-321-2211.
Exclusively for the friends and associates of: **Mr. D. Kennedy** 272543104	*Exclusively for the friends and associates of:* **Mr. D. Kennedy** 272543104
USED BY: Name (PLEASE PRINT)_____ Address _____	*USED BY:* Name (PLEASE PRINT)_____ Address _____
Redeem before 12/30/89; only one coupon per stay. Free weekend night must be taken by 4/1/90, rooms offered are standard Courtyard rooms and subject to availability. Does not apply with other offers and discounts. No coupon facsimiles accepted.	Redeem before 12/30/89; only one coupon per stay. Free weekend night must be taken by 4/1/90, rooms offered are standard Courtyard rooms and subject to availability. Does not apply with other offers and discounts. No coupon facsimiles accepted.

Reprinted courtesy of Marriott Courtyard.

DIRECT MARKETING ASSOCIATION, INC.
6 East 43rd Street * New York, NY 10017 * 212-689-4077 * Telex 22 0560

Dear DMA Member:

I'd like to ask you to look through your Rolodex or address book and come up with the name of at least one person who probably isn't a DMA member, but who you believe should be.

You see, we're embarking on a new membership enrollment campaign at the DMA. And the logical place to start is with you. I know that you have many contacts both in and outside the direct marketing industry. And you know what DMA does for you and your counterparts in all kinds of direct marketing organizations who use direct marketing techniques. Surely, you know someone who would benefit from DMA membership but who for one reason or another may not be aware of what the DMA has to offer. And, if you can help us build the number of people in your segment, we'll be able to offer even more services to you.

I'd appreciate it if you'd send that person's name, address and phone number to me. Because I'd like to talk to him or her about joining the DMA before the year is up.

For your convenience, I've enclosed a form on which you can list the name of your nominee. I'd also like to know if you'd permit me to use your name when I make the actual contact. So I've included a check-off box to that effect on the form as well. Obviously, we will respect your wishes.

I appreciate your taking the time from your busy schedule to help us. I look forward to receiving your nomination and soon hope to add your referral to our membership roles.

Sincerely,

Michael Faulkner
Vice President
Membership Development

P.S. You may wish to consider an associate who is presently not in direct marketing or who may only be using it to a limited extent. As our industry grows, they are among those people most likely to need our services.

Reprinted courtesy of Direct Marketing Associates, Inc.

5. To Introduce New Products or Services to Present or Past Clients

If there is one universal discovery I've made with every business I've ever consulted with—small or large, local or global, industrial or consumer-targeted, product- or service-oriented, it is that they all underutilize their own customer mailing lists. (Some don't even maintain such a list!)

I have a simple premise and a simpler plan for increasing just about any business's sales through the use of sales letters. First, the premise: it is easier to sell more to customers who know you, like you, and trust you than it is to get more new customers. The first sale is the toughest; the established customer is predisposed to purchase from you again. Second, the method: develop and mail a new sales letter to all your customers each and every month, introducing a new product or service.

Let me point out, by the way, that if a product or service is new to the customer, it's new, period. I have one client who sells a variety of products to hospitals and clinics. We broke his customer lists down by what people had bought and what they hadn't bought. Even though he sells about a hundred different items, most customers were buyers of only three or four. So we created a complex program of single-product sales letters sent to nonbuyers of those products. If you bought Product A, you got a letter about a product you hadn't bought—say, Product B. But if you were a user of B and had never bought A, you got the letter about A. These letters have been consistently pulling a 2% to 3% order rate and averaging $1 of gross profit per letter mailed. Think about that! If every sales letter you mail reliably brings back at least $1 of profit, what do you do? Right—mail as many as you can!

THE PET FOOD SUPERSTORE
123 Dog Street
City, State, Zip

Dear Customer,

SAVE 50% ON NEW SUPER-ANTI-TICK SHAMPOO
JUST RIGHT FOR THE COMING SUMMER SEASON

We appreciate your business; we appreciate having you as a customer! Now, thanks to a special arrangement with the DOG CARE PRODUCTS COMPANY, we have an opportunity to say "Thanks!" with a very special, timely offer:

The enclosed brochure fully explains DOG CARE'S new SUPER-ANTI-TICK SHAMPOO and ANTI-TICK COLLAR products. You'll do your dog and your family a favor by putting these products to use before the start of the summer tick season, in just a few weeks. Right now, you can get a $1/2$-quart bottle of the Shampoo and the Collar at half-price . . . you save $9.95! . . . you pay only $9.95. And you can order by mail or phone, and use your Visa or MasterCard if you like. We'll set the products aside here at the store for you or we'll ship them out, right to your door at no extra charge!

Call us today at 258-DOGG!

Your Friends At The Superstore!

6. To Sell Directly by Mail Order

Yes, mail order is a huge subject in and of itself that cannot be covered here. I would only like to point out that many nonmail order firms can still generate some business purely through sales letters.

Earlier in this book I showed you how a Las Vegas hotel marketed "vacation packages" via sales letters.

If you have regular, repeat customers, there's probably a way for you to obtain reorders and stimulate additional purchases from them with periodic sales letters.

An example of an "ordinary business" using a sales letter to sell directly by mail appears on the facing page.

7. To Reduce Refunds Via Post-Purchase Reassurance

Salespeople are familiar with "buyer's remorse": someone may buy something on impulse, then a day or two later begin to feel bad about the purchase. Maybe the product isn't exactly what the buyer thought it was, maybe the problem has nothing to do with the product but a lot to do with having spent the money. Regardless of the reason, buyer's remorse can lead to refunds.

A good sales letter—with a congratulatory theme—sent to the customer the day after the purchase can make the sale stick.

On the following pages is an example of such a letter, developed for a self- improvement program sold via cable TV. Use of this letter, sent separately from the product, significantly reduced returns. Couldn't the same type of letter help with any product, service, or transaction where buyer's remorse can set in?

Hello again!

By now you should already be deeply involved in your **THINK AND GROW RICH SUCCESS SYSTEM.** So I wanted to write and add my personal words of encouragement—and issue you a special challenge.

First, let me re-emphasize: I believe you now have the very best program of its kind in existence. By listening to the audio-cassettes repeatedly (as you commute to and from work, for example), you'll find yourself automatically "getting in tune" with the thinking, the attitudes, the convictions necessary to win big in life! And by studying the book and utilizing the other course materials as directed, you'll master the principles and discover Napoleon Hill's great success secret that much sooner.

Let me also encourage you to give some time to studying your bonus **THINK AND GROW RICH** Business Reports and listening to the accompanying audiocassettes, which were prepared exclusively for you. Whether you want to start a business from scratch, buy a going business, buy a franchise, or more effectively promote your present enterprise, these reports provide "nuts and bolts" information you can put to work right now. Even if you don't yet see yourself as an entrepreneur, you can use the guidelines in the report on Winning Career Strategies to begin moving ahead. And the report entitled How to Gain Control of Your Finances may well be worth the entire price of admission!

Altogether, this system gives you a winning game plan. So now—as my coaches used to tell me—all you've got to do is execute! And that brings me to the second thing I wanted to talk with you about: the temptation to quit.

Even though this **THINK AND GROW RICH SUCCESS SYSTEM** has been wonderfully designed to help you master the principles as easily as possible, it still requires some dedication and persistent effort on your part.

Do you remember the old bromide, "Quitters never win and winners never quit?" Well, with that in mind, I'm going to say something now that may shock you: we're all quitters! And the sooner we realize it, the better. Then we can get on with the business of overcoming it.

Let me tell you about the time I quit.

It was in my next-to-last year in football, the 1977–78 season. With me as quarterback the year before, the Vikings had lost their third Super Bowl. The Minnesota fans had decided that Tarkenton had to go. People came up to me on the streets and in restaurants to tell me just that!

Our third game of the new season was against the Tampa Bay Buccaneers, then a two-year-old expansion team that had lost every game the previous year. Now they were in Minnesota playing the mighty Vikings, but we were losing in the fourth quarter!

Our great team had gotten a little older. We were struggling. In that fourth quarter, I think all 47,000 people in the stadium stood up and booed me. I'll never forget that day. I had suffered some mighty booing during my final season with the New York Giants in 1971, but nothing hurt as much as the sound of those Viking fans calling for my head on a platter. I came off the field that day more depressed and angry than I had ever been.

The next morning I walked into Coach Bud Grant's office and said, "I'm going home to Atlanta and I'm not coming back." I was quitting after the third game of the season.

The next day Bud called me in Atlanta. I said, "I've thought about it and I'm still quitting."

Bud replied, "Fran, I wish I had some magic word to tell you that would make you come back and play. But I don't. I just hope you understand that if you don't come back, we have no chance to make the playoffs this year."

Now that really hit me!

I thought to myself, "You selfish son of a gun! Here you have 44 teammates out there. Old Tinglehoff and Marshall are up there busting their backsides. They're old and tired and they're still trying. But just because you get booed, you're going to run off and throw their chances to the wolves."

After I hung up, I packed my bags, got the next plane back to Minneapolis, and never said a word to anyone. I just showed up for Wednesday practice. Most people never knew I had quit.

The important thing to recognize is that winners are people who sometimes have the desire to quit, but *they develop ways of dealing with it.* And that's what **THINK AND GROW RICH** is all about.

Why have I told you this story?

Because you'll probably be tempted to quit, too. Maybe you'll listen to the tapes for a little while and not see any miraculous changes in your life, so you'll feel like quitting. Sometimes we're a little too "instant"-oriented these days. Maybe you'll try some new venture and "get your nose bloodied," and feel like quitting. I want you to know that, as far as I'm concerned, it's perfectly okay to feel like quitting now and then—<u>as long as you don't</u>!

I really want to see you take this winning **THINK AND GROW RICH** game plan and execute! That's why I'm excited about offering you this little challenge and reward:

Whenever you're ready, send in a list of the 25 most valuable ideas you've gained from your study of this THINK AND GROW RICH SYSTEM. Tell us how you've benefited from these ideas. We'll then send you a suitable-for-framing Certificate of Completion with Dr. Napoleon Hill's picture and his famous quotation, "Anything the mind can conceive and believe, it can achieve"; my photograph; and the signatures of myself and Mr. W. Clement Stone, the president of the Napoleon Hill Foundation.

I hope you'll be proud to hang this beautiful certificate in a prominent place in your home or office, where you'll see it often and be reminded that anything <u>you</u> can conceive and believe, <u>you</u> can achieve!

In closing, let me congratulate you once again on investing in this tested and proven program of self-development and achievement.

Believe me, I meet people all the time who <u>wish</u> for greater success, but I meet far fewer who, like <u>you</u>, are willing to do something about it.

Sincerely,

Fran Tarkenton

P.S. I've enclosed, as an extra gift from the publisher, two 25% discount certificates. Each may be used toward the purchase of any of the other fine programs offered in the **THINK AND GROW RICH BUSINESS REPORTS**. To me, winning is a daily proposition, something you're always learning to do better. For this reason, you'll undoubtedly want to add some of these other excellent programs to your success library.

8. For All Sorts of Business and Personal Correspondence and Communication

We spend the lion's share of our lives selling! You have to sell yourself and your ideas to superiors, subordinates, associates, stockholders, vendors, and countless others every day. Actually, very little communication takes place without the intent of persuading.

Whether you need to write a letter to a customer or a supplier, to your stockholders, to the banker, to your son's or daughter's school principal, or to your senator, you'll be attempting to sell at least a viewpoint, if not something significantly more tangible than that.

The principles behind this system, then, apply to every type of persuasive communication. Studied and used, these techniques will make you a much more effective communicator.

SECTION IV

The Million-Dollar Sales Letter Secret: The Power of a Sequence

One of the biggest mistakes most marketers make is doing "one-shot mailings." Simply put, it takes repetition to have impact. But I advise against Madison Avenue's extraordinarily slow, patient, plodding, expensive version of repetition, with results sloppily measured by market-share movement or brand recognition over long periods of time. Instead, I most often work with a tight, timed sequence over a 45- to 60-day period, capable of quickly creating brand/message recognition as well as considerable, immediate response.

In this section, I've reprinted a series of my sales letters for a chain of Italian restaurants that has literally become famous; I've used it in all my seminars for nearly 10 years, and shown it to well over 2 million people. For years, the only way to get this "model" was in my Magnetic Marketing System,* for $399 or more. Not only do these letters include many of the tactics presented throughout this book, but they demonstrate how to structure a multistep mailing sequence. After you read these sample letters, ask yourself this simple question: do you have any doubt that, in any household receiving these letters, Giorgio's is not a topic of conversation?

Of course, people who sell "sophisticated" stuff to "sophisticated" people will quickly insist they could never use something like this. They're very wrong. You *can* separate style from structure. The humorous style helps whether selling million-dollar computer systems to CEOs in the boardroom or carpet cleaning to folks in their living rooms. But the structure is absolutely proven to be universally effective. Often, the response from the second and third letters combined will double the response obtained from the first. Sometimes, even better.

---

*My Magnetic Marketing System and Tool Kit with over 200 letters and letter sequence examples is available at 1-800-223-7180 or *www.kimble-kennedypublishing.com.*

I call this my "million-dollar secret" because the creation of sales letter *sequences* rather than just creating sales letters is as responsible as any other, single idea for my becoming a millionaire while still young enough to enjoy it, and for making millions and millions of dollars for my personal clients. As secrets go, I suppose it's not much of one. Frankly, I "stole" it from the collection industry; the Giorgio's letters, for example, are very closely modeled after a basic sequence of dunning letters—first notice, second notice, third notice. But very, very few marketers know to use this tactic or have the discipline to use it, so it's just as valuable as a bona-fide secret.

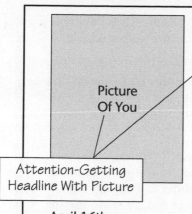

Picture Of You

| Attention-Getting Headline With Picture |

A Confidential Letter to the Husband of the House from Giorgio

—Romance Director Giorgio's Italian Grotto

"She may be waiting . . . just anticipating . . . things she may never possess . . . but while she's waiting, try a little tenderness . . ."

April 16th

Dear Husband,

| Problem |

Women are different than we are. (Vive le difference!) YOUR loving wife needs, wants, and deserves SPECIAL ATTENTION maybe more often than you think to give it to her.

| Agitate Problem |

You are busy. Preoccupied with work. Aggravated with that dumb-dumb that you have to deal with every day at the office. Tired. Who has time or the energy to even think about "romance?" (Two-thirds of all marriages end in divorce and the number-one reason given by divorcing women—"he just didn't pay enough attention to me anymore.")

| "To the Rescue" Solution |

For you, my friend, I have got a SOLUTION!

With this letter, YOU are entitled to an evening charmed by all the creativity of Giorgio, the Official Romance Director!

| Create Vivid Word Pictures that Appeal to the Senses! |

When you and your Very-Significant-Other arrive at Giorgio's, you'll be ushered to the special dining room lit only by candlelight and the roaring fire in the fireplace . . . with the view of the sunset or starry night over the harbor! (When you make your reservation, I will GUARANTEE your choice of a near-the-fireplace or window-side table!)

In this undercrowded, intimate dining room there will be NO families, NO CHILDREN, NO disruptions. Quiet mood music. A peaceful environment. A haven from the hustle, bustle, noise, and pushing and shoving and rushing of the real world.

On your table, in a crystal bud vase, there will be a single dewy-fresh red rose for your lady. (It and the vase are hers to take home.)

We will begin with a carafe of our wonderful house Italian wine—red or white, your choice—compliments of Giorgio! And fresh baked, piping hot, lightly garlic-buttered, crusty Italian breadsticks.

For dinner, all the TENDERNESS the two of you can handle—if you choose the specialty of the house: an entree of melt-in-your-mouth tender veal on a bed of angel hair pasta, with a to-die-for pesto sauce . . . or your choice of five other wonderful entrees.

> Really Make Them See, Smell, and Taste It!

Any choice from our dessert tray . . .

Espresso . . .

And finally a heart-shaped box with four delicate, Italian gelato filled chocolates presented to your lady with a flourish!

Now, is that an evening to enjoy, to luxuriate in, to remember? Will that make you a hero? Ah—Giorgio GUARANTEES it.

We can only accommodate twelve couples each evening with this very special Romance Dinner, so it's important to call and make reservations as early as you can. Ask for me—Giorgio—Noon to 10:00 P.M. (or stop in for our Businessman's lunch). See me, and make these Romance arrangements personally. I'm the handsome-looking devil in the deep blue tuxedo jacket, in the lounge.

> Limited Number Available

Awaiting your commands—to make 'a magic for you!

Giorgio.

P.S. The cost? EVERYTHING, the entire Romance Dinner for two exactly as I've described it—just $59.95. If you wish you can even pay in advance with VISA, MASTERCARD, AMERICAN EXPRESS, or CARTE BLANCHE and not be troubled by a check the evening you are here.

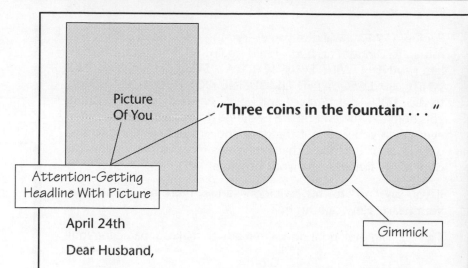

Picture Of You

"Three coins in the fountain . . . "

Attention-Getting Headline With Picture

Gimmick

April 24th

Dear Husband,

As you can see, I've attached 3 shiny pennies to this letter. I've done this for two important reasons: first, to grab your attention for just a moment or two or three. Second, to remind you of that wonderful romantic song "Three Coins in the Fountain . . ."

You see, this is your second notice . . . your romance wake-up call from me, Giorgio!, the Romance Director at Giorgio's Italian Grotto. My bell tolls—does it toll for thee?

Problem

It is a stress-filled, busy, hectic, tough, tiring, demanding, mind-numbing, energy-sapping battle each and every day out there, isn't it? I know—after all, I am a businessman too. (And a husband too—married to my beautiful Isabella for 25 years.) It is easy, tempting, even natural to come home to "the cave" after a day of doing battle, shove the rock onto the doorway, and collapse onto the couch. BUT WITHOUT FREQUENT ROMANCE, THE FLAME FLICKERS AND DIES. You know that, deep-down inside—but who has the time and energy to create romance?

Giorgio to the rescue!!!

Agitate Problem

You know, I am deeply disappointed that I didn't hear from you after my first letter and invitation to let me create a truly romantic, memorable evening for you and your lady. So, I am here again, this time with an EVEN BETTER INVITATION . . . a truly remarkable offer . . .

For just $59.95, I will give you everything I described before, the romantic Dinner For Two—listed again, at the bottom of this letter—AND I WILL EVEN SEND A "STRETCH," GLEAMING WHITE, FULLY-EQUIPPED LIMOUSINE RIGHT TO YOUR HOME to pick YOU—the "Prince" and your "Princess" up—and bring you home at the end of the evening! (Imagine the look in her eyes when you walk out the door and, instead of going to the garage, your tuxedoed chauffeur steps forward and opens the door of the limousine for your lady to enter!)

If you say "no" to this invitation—ah, is there no romance in your heart? How can this be?

Call ME, Giorgio!, right now. I'm ready to make 'a magic for you!

> Giorgio.
> With a song in his heart.

HERE IS EVERYTHING INCLUDED FOR THE INCREDIBLE LOW PRICE OF JUST $59.95:

Irresistible Offer

SECTION V

"High-Tech" Sales Letters

When I wrote the first edition of this book in 1991, very few marketers were using broadcast fax or fax-on-demand, and Internet sites, auto-responders, and e-mail were unknowns. Since then, of course, virtually every office and many homes have been equipped with fax machines. Millions of people use the Internet. E-commerce is rapidly growing. All this prompts plenty of questions about how my "Ultimate Sales Letter Techniques" apply to these tech-media. Fortunately, the answer is: very well!

1. The Fax Machine

These days, lists of fax numbers are just as readily available as mailing lists. And, although there are legal issues you ought to consider, the use of "broadcast fax"—mass faxing—is a very popular and, quite often, very effective marketing tool. Just for example, I've developed a complete campaign of sales letters delivered by fax for a client who sells term life insurance to doctors, architects, airline pilots, and other specialized prospect groups—and we are selling millions of dollars of life insurance with no salespeople and no telemarketing.

For most purposes, faxed sales letters need to be kept to only one or two pages, and thus are best used to generate leads, not to make sales or even to secure appointments. But other than restricting the length, every suggestion, tactic, and example presented in this book applies perfectly to the sales letter prepared for delivery by fax, from what I said about headlines all the way through to what I said about ease of response.

2. Fax-on-Demand

This is simply an automated way of delivering sales letters and other literature to prospects or customers requesting them, with no delay, no handling, and no printing and postage costs. Here, there are no real length limitations, any more than there are with sales letters delivered by mail. The drawback is that you can't use colors, photos may not fax clearly, you can't vary the size, color, and texture of the paper, and so forth. The advantages are speed and cost. In many instances, the trade-off is acceptable. And again, every single guideline presented in this book applies to the sales letters you would store in an FOD system, for delivery via fax-on-demand.

3. Internet Sites

You certainly can put even a lengthy sales letter up on a Web site and have it work for you there, and/or be downloaded by interested prospects. Among other things you'll find at my Web site, *www.dankennedy.com*, is the complete sales letter for my *No B.S. Marketing Letter*, and it works very well. You do not need to fear "long copy" here any more than in printed pieces; seriously interested prospects want a lot of information. (The average time spent at my site by each visitor is 17 to 25 minutes.)

4. Auto-responders

This technology is somewhat similar to fax-on-demand. Web site visitors can request and have sent to them information computer to computer. You can also preprogram the sending of a sequence of e-mails; for example, 24 hours, then 72 hours, then 5, 10, and 15 days after a prospect has visited your site, all done for you—"look Ma, no hands!"

5. E-mail

If sending a requested sales letter via e-mail, length is still not an issue. If sending unasked-for follow-up e-mails like I just described, brevity is required. The best technique I know is a brief e-mail giving reason for the prospect to return to the Web site for newly posted information—then do your selling there.

However, most of the sales letter strategies presented in this book apply even to these brief e-mails. For example, the "RE" line on the e-mail should be a compelling headline.

A warning: a lot of the people selling the services of con-structing Web sites, doing e-mail marketing, etc., are "techies" with little or no sales or marketing savvy or experience. They are at least as dangerous as graphic artists, if not more so. You need to carefully separate their valid advice on technical matters from their invalid advice on marketing matters. Contrary to what many of these tech-types will insist, a strong sales letter is a strong sales letter is a strong sales letter regardless of the delivery medium being used. "What works" does *not* change significantly whether carving it on a rock, having it put on papyrus by a calligrapher, or posting it on a Web site.

ABOUT CONTACTING
THE AUTHOR

The author, Dan Kennedy, is available for a limited number of speaking engagements and consulting assignments. He also edits and publishes *The No B.S. Marketing Letter.* For information:

Fax: 1–602–269–3113
Online: *www.dankennedy.com*

For a catalog of other books, manuals, audiocassettes, and marketing tool kits by Dan Kennedy, contact Kimble & Kennedy Publishing at 1–800–223–7180 or *www.kimble-kennedypublishing.com.*

RECOMMENDED BOOKS LIST

Secrets of Closing the Sale by Zig Ziglar
High Impact Selling by William Brooks
No B.S. Sales Success by Dan Kennedy
The Closers
Sales Closing Power by J. Douglas Edwards

---

*These books and an expanded Recommended Reading List are available at *www.dankennedy.com.*

INDEX